FLEUR BEALE has been writing for over thirty years, has twice been awarded the Gaelyn Gordon Award for a much loved book and has been short-listed several times for the NZ Post Children and Young Adults Book Awards. When she was asked if she'd be interested in writing *Sins of the Father*, she didn't hesitate as she's always been captured by stories where people are subjected to control of one sort or another. The genesis for her 1998 book *I am not Esther* (2009 recipient of the Gaelyn Gordon Award) came from hearing of a young man who had been thrown out of a fundamentalist sect for non-compliance.

She lives in Wellington, dividing her time between writing, assessing manuscripts, visiting schools as part of the Writers in Schools scheme, and travelling to visit her two adult daughters overseas.

Proceeds from the sale of *Sins of the Father* will go towards the establishment of a charitable trust. This trust will assist individuals and families who leave the Gloriavale community and wish to be repatriated into society.

Sins of the Father is based on actual events, however in some cases names and timelines have been altered for confidentiality purposes.

ISBN: 978 1 877460 30 2

All photographs and home movie stills are from the Cooper family collection unless otherwise stated. Every effort has been made to trace and contact copyright holders.

First published by Longacre Press, 2009
30 Moray Place, Dunedin, New Zealand
Reprinted 2009

A catalogue record for this book is available from the National Library of New Zealand.

Book design by Christine Buess
Cover design by Nick Wright/Christine Buess
Cover image courtesy Melanie Reid/TV3
Printed by Astra Print, Wellington

www.longacre.co.nz

SINS OF THE FATHER

THE LONG SHADOW OF A RELIGIOUS CULT
A NEW ZEALAND STORY

FLEUR BEALE

Longacre Press

CONTENTS

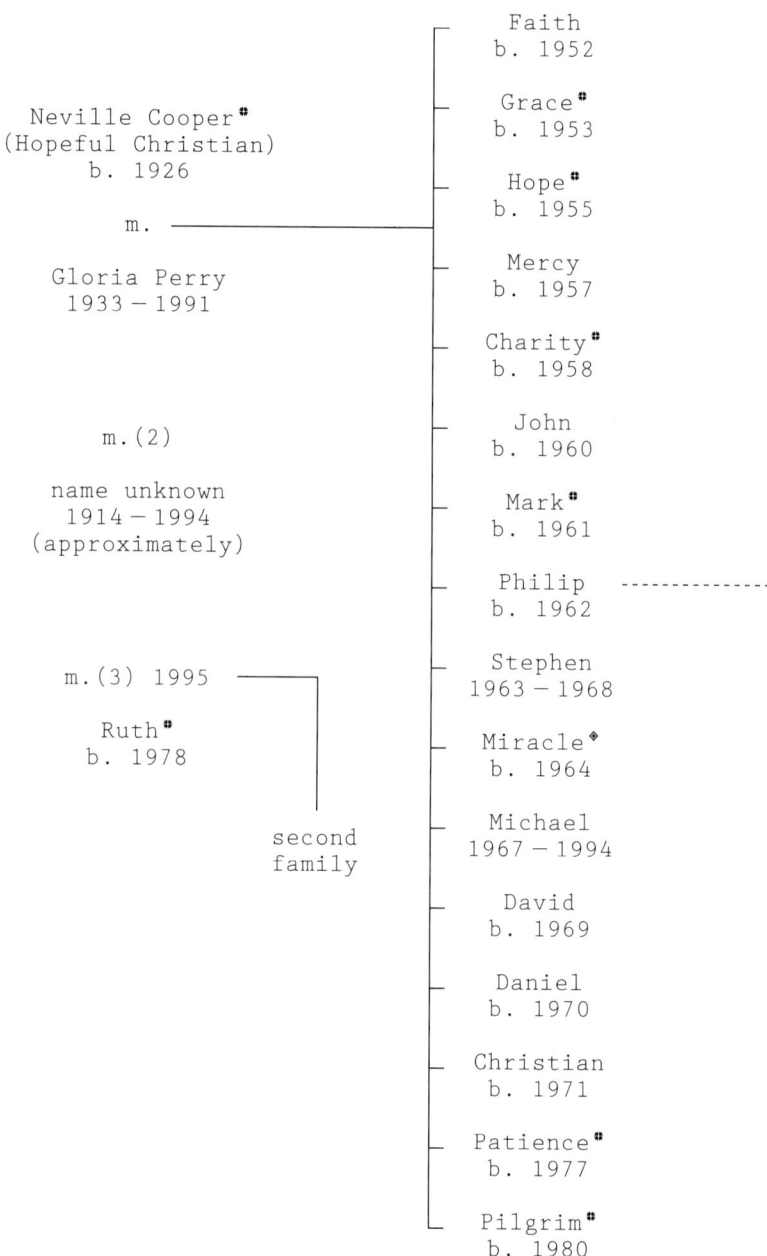

Neville Cooper [#]
(Hopeful Christian)
b. 1926

m. ───────────────

Gloria Perry
1933 — 1991

m.(2)

name unknown
1914 — 1994
(approximately)

m.(3) 1995 ───────

Ruth [#]
b. 1978

second
family

Faith
b. 1952

Grace [#]
b. 1953

Hope [#]
b. 1955

Mercy
b. 1957

Charity [#]
b. 1958

John
b. 1960

Mark [#]
b. 1961

Philip ─────────────
b. 1962

Stephen
1963 — 1968

Miracle [◆]
b. 1964

Michael
1967 — 1994

David
b. 1969

Daniel
b. 1970

Christian
b. 1971

Patience [#]
b. 1977

Pilgrim [#]
b. 1980

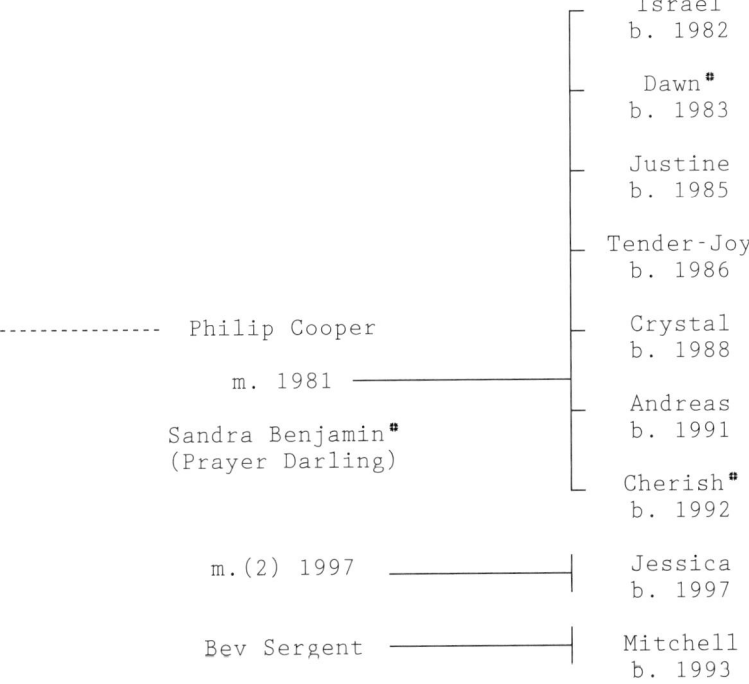

Israel
b. 1982

Dawn #
b. 1983

Justine
b. 1985

Tender-Joy
b. 1986

Philip Cooper

Crystal
b. 1988

m. 1981

Andreas
b. 1991

Sandra Benjamin #
(Prayer Darling)

Cherish #
b. 1992

m.(2) 1997

Jessica
b. 1997

Bev Sergent

Mitchell
b. 1993

Still living in Gloriavale.

◆ Miracle and her husband Perry live at nearby
Lake Brunner but are still part of the community.

7

New Zealand

N

TARANAKI

New Plymouth

Wanganui

Marlborough Sounds

Nelson   Picton
                Wellington

Westport   Blenheim

M A R L B O R O U G H

Greymouth   L Haupiri   Kaikoura
                    'Gloriavale'
Hokitika   L Brunner

            Arthur's Pass
SOUTH ISLAND   'Springbank'
                        Cust   Rangiora
Franz Josef   S O U T H E R N   A L P S   Christchurch

                C A N T E R B U R Y

Haast   W E S T L A N D   L Tekapo   Ashburton

        M A C K E N Z I E   C O U N T R Y   Timaru

                            100km

Queenstown

            O T A G O   Oamaru

        Dunedin

INTRODUCTION

At the age of 27, father of five, Phil Cooper, walked away from the religious community his father Neville had created and still controls 20 years later. This is Phil's story and the story of his seven children, their mother Sandra, and their struggles to live in a family that's split between the outside world and what is now called the Gloriavale Christian Community.

Early in his life, Phil had no choice about belonging to the strict, fundamentalist religious cult. His father required obedience from his children and Phil was a young teenager when Neville began the process of drawing his followers apart from the world.

Neville first established his community in rural Springbank in Canterbury, near the small township of Cust. Followers were attracted by his growing reputation as a charismatic preacher and a true man of God. Gradually he pulled them away from mainstream religious practice. By the late 1980s all were living communally in purpose-built accommodation on the small farm owned by his eldest daughter and her husband.

Within a few years, the community had bought hundreds of hectares of land at Haupiri on the West Coast, inland from Greymouth. Neville called this property Gloriavale in honour of his wife Gloria who died in 1991. When an adjoining farm was bought he called it Glen Hopeful after himself, having changed his name by deed poll from Neville Cooper to Hopeful Christian.

Phil left the community late in 1989 while it was still at Springbank and not as isolated as at remote Haupiri. Gloriavale, now twice the size of the founding community, has developed somewhat different structures to organise its 400 people. Gloriavale owns considerably more land and operates a variety of industries. It is not known whether the dark history of the Springbank days is being repeated in Gloriavale. People who have connections with it believe not; Phil hopes they are right.

In 2008 Phil and Israel, his eldest son, decided it was time to tell their story, and I was approached to help them do it.

FLEUR BEALE

What We Believe was written and published by the Christian Church at Springbank, First edition, The Eight Month, 1989. The book, researched and written by Fervent Stedfast who is second in command of Gloriavale, sets out the way its members should live, what they should believe, and how they should behave. It has the same importance as the Bible and is Neville Cooper's interpretation of the Bible.

PREFACE

by Israel Cooper

Many of the stories told in these pages are of our childhood. We have tried to be as accurate as possible but we realize that memory is an elusive thing. The broad strokes are what happened and the details are as true as we could make them.

My early life was spent in an environment where people willingly surrendered their freedom of choice to my grandfather, ceding to this powerful and charismatic evangelist the power to chart the course of their lives. Our family history, including as it does wrecked lives as well as stories of triumph, testifies to the preciousness of the freedom to choose one's own path. My brothers, sisters, and I never take our own freedom of choice for granted.

We have learned that the most powerful thing we can do is to make a conscious decision not to repeat the mistakes of the past. In the world, this is what makes heroes. It changes destinies and transforms generations. In a single moment, a single choice can stop thousands of years of history repeating. It can change lives, restore families, and bring prosperity. It is a wonderful and powerful gift to have.

My single biggest concern with the Gloriavale Christian Community and its predecessor at Springbank where I spent the first years of my life, is that it takes away or limits that freedom. Through fear it removes freedom of choice, the ability to choose your destiny, the opportunity to fail and learn from your mistakes, and most importantly, to be able to choose to love unconditionally.

For giving me that most powerful gift of freedom I will always be incredibly thankful to my father. Knowing how precious this gift is, and the price that both my parents have paid for it, has awakened me to the power and responsibility I now have. I can choose justice or mercy; I can choose to forgive. I can choose to make my life happy and fulfilled; I can choose to love and be loved.

Most importantly I can choose to end the sins of my father and my father's father, and I can choose to give the gift of choice, its possibilities and responsibilities, to my own son.

Neither I nor my siblings want another generation to have to endure the consequences of the heartbreaking decisions our own parents were forced to make. Both of them believed utterly in the rightness of their decisions and we honour, respect and love them for having the courage to act in accordance with their beliefs.

I wish too to honour our mother's integrity for making a decision she believed with her heart and soul to be the only one she could make for the salvation of her children. She lost the freedom to be our mother, but her daily prayers that we would find faith have not been in vain. Perhaps paradoxically we have come to our faith because of the decisions both our parents made.

To Mum, Dawn and Cherish; our story may already
be half written, but the future is still ours to write.
One day we will be in each others' arms again.
Love from your family.

CHAPTER ONE: BEGINNINGS

Christian children should honour and obey their Christian parents in all things. This they should do all the days of their lives, even when they themselves become adults.
WHAT WE BELIEVE, P. 69

Phil Cooper was 11 years old when he began to understand that his father meant to bend him to his will. Over 30 years later, the memory of what happened that day is sharp and clear.

The family was on holiday in Queenstown, and the setting was idyllic with the lake reflecting the mountains and the jewel-blue sky. It was the first holiday in years for the large Cooper family and Phil had looked forward to it for weeks, saving up his pocket money to spend in the shops. The Cooper kids didn't normally go much further afield than their home in Rangiora in Canterbury where their father Neville preached and headed his ministry, so for Phil the prospect of going to the shops and spending his 20 dollars was as exciting as going to Disneyland.

The family arrived in Queenstown, settled in to the caravan and Neville decided to give his wife a rest: he would cook the dinner. He gathered up three of his sons. 'Let's go shopping, boys.'

They got to the butchery but Neville didn't have enough money so he turned to Phil. 'Son, have you got any money?'

Phil told him no, he didn't. What happened next will stay with him forever.

Neville said, 'Yes you have. You're a selfish little boy.' He pushed his son away from him. 'You are not part of this family.'

Phil burst into tears and tore out of the shop. He had no idea where he was going, not even what he was doing. He ended up sitting down at the wharf, sobbing. After a while he went looking for his dad, found him walking along with the other two boys, and handed over all his money. Neville took it without saying a word. Phil had complied with his father's will and was accepted back into the family.

For Phil, the incident revealed where he stood in relation to his dad, and part of him knew even then that he'd have to stand on his own feet if he wanted to survive, that he would have to separate himself from his father. The scene remains one of his most vivid memories. *You are not part of this family* still plays in his head, and he can still see himself running.

From that time on, he began to dream of freedom. The harsh discipline of his life was nothing new, but that incident caused him to examine his position with regard to his father. It was a defining moment, the first of many incidents revealing that his father's love was conditional on total obedience.

Neville had always been a strict disciplinarian, and harder on his sons than his daughters. Faith, the eldest of the 15 children who survived to adulthood, loved and admired him. He didn't speak much about his own Australian childhood, only telling his children that he'd had to leave school at 12 to work in his father's fruit shop. Mr Cooper senior was a hard man, who threw Neville out of home when he was 16, probably as a consequence of the clash of two strong personalities. Neville stayed more or less estranged from his family thereafter, and although his mother visited regularly when Neville and his own family lived in Queensland, his children never had anything to do with their two aunts or heard much about their father's brother who was killed in World War Two. Neville also served in the armed forces, joining the air force at some stage, but didn't serve overseas since the war finished before his training was completed.

The family mythology is of the young Neville running out of control, or at least living a less-than-desirable lifestyle until he was 21, when he experienced his conversion to Christianity. He seems to have been in steady work as an apprentice panel beater, and he was a keen sportsman, becoming a talented rugby league player despite his short stature.

His children don't know the circumstances surrounding their father's conversion to Christianity but they do know that the experience was profound and life changing. He became a regular church-goer which is how he met Gloria, a quiet, gentle girl whom he married in 1949 when she was 16 and he 21. Faith, the first of their 16 children, was born in 1952, and was followed quickly by four more daughters all named for the virtues: Grace, Hope, Mercy and Charity.

Neville became a preacher at the age of 23 and set himself up as a travelling evangelist in order to bring the word of God to as many people as possible. He was young, bounding with energy, utterly convinced of his beliefs, and so charismatic that he swept people along with the power and conviction of his message. He was a hellfire-and-brimstone preacher whose mission was to rid the world of sin. Bringing the word of God to the masses was what mattered to him and he lived his beliefs, espousing strong moral and family values. He preached from a marquee, calling his ministry the Voice of Deliverance, and as his reputation as a dynamic evangelist grew, the invitations to speak increased. He would pack up the marquee and drive, or later pilot his own plane, to venues throughout New South Wales and Queensland.

Life for Gloria can't have been easy. Her husband was a good provider but he didn't have a steady job because he was away preaching, sometimes for weeks at a time, on his tent campaigns. She would be alone with her young family and solely responsible for supervising their correspondence schooling. She would not have complained or even wished for things to be different. It was her duty as a wife to be subservient to her husband, obey his commands, and bear and care for his children.

When he was home, Neville would take any paid work he could find, panel beating when it was available but something else if it wasn't. During a stint as a sewing machine salesman he taught himself to sew, using this skill at home to make pretty dresses for his small daughters.

In those early years, the family moved house regularly, sometimes in response to churches inviting Neville to do speaking tours, and sometimes because he had fallen out with the pastor of the local church Gloria and the children were attending.

By June 1959, Neville had completed converting an old bus into a three-roomed home in which he meant to tour Australia, but three days after Faith's seventh birthday disaster struck. It was winter, but the bus was warm and baby Charity was tucked up in the bedroom at the rear. Much to the delight of the four older girls, the pet rabbit was hopping around the floor of the living room, but suddenly it knocked against the heater, spilling kerosene onto the floor. Gloria grabbed a cloth to clean it up, but the friction must have ignited a spark: the rabbit caught fire and fled, tearing around the small room, setting alight furnishings as it tried to escape. The place was an inferno, with the door to the back room where the baby was asleep impassable. Neville and Gloria grabbed the four older girls, and raced outside where Neville hammered at the rear window till it smashed and he was able to snatch the baby to safety.

The family were now destitute, with no money, no belongings, and only the clothes they were wearing. A church in Maryborough north of Brisbane heard of their plight and invited Neville there to preach. They had a house available for his family, too. This was the furthest the family had ever moved, but at least they had nothing to pack and arrived at their new home unencumbered by luggage. Immediately Neville found work and began the slow process of building up their belongings again, alongside his preaching schedule. Soon after their arrival, he went to an auction hoping to buy cheap furniture for their bare home, but an old piano caught his eye. Despite arguing with himself that a piano didn't feature on his list of essentials, there was something compelling about it and by the end of the day he found himself owning the ancient, battered instrument. He got it home and for some reason opened the back, where he discovered a wad of bank notes. By the look of them they'd been there for years and there were a lot of them – 800 pounds in all. It was a fortune but Neville was a scrupulously honest man and so made strenuous efforts to track down the rightful owner. The auction house told him the piano had come from a deceased estate, and no, there were no heirs. That wasn't enough for Neville and he tried for several months to find somebody legally entitled to the money. When nobody came forward, he finally accepted that it was his and used it to set up his family.

The association with the Maryborough church didn't last. It's unclear now what caused the breakdown, but Faith suspects there was probably wrong on both sides. In 1962 Neville moved his family to Brisbane where they lived in a war pension house. By now Gloria had given birth to John and Mark, with Philip born shortly after the move to Brisbane.

The pattern of moving house continued. In each new area Neville would find a suitable church for his family to join, usually Four Square or Assembly of God congregations, which he, too, would attend when he was at home. By now his reputation as an inspirational preacher had spread throughout Australia and New Zealand. He left his family for three months when he was invited to tour New Zealand, and as had happened in Australia, crowds clamoured to hear his vision of a world based on biblical foundations.

Back home, he continued to preach, interspersing his campaigns with periods of paid work when he would accompany his family to their church. But he was a man ahead of his time, and would try to force his own ideas on the pastor, as well as challenging the man's doctrine. Once the inevitable split came, he would move his family on to a new location, settle them in to another church and the pattern would repeat, usually within 18 months.

Faith's memories of her father are happy ones. When she and her sisters were small, he would brush and plait their hair. He taught her to read and write and as she grew older she would go with him to panel beating jobs where she learnt the basics of the trade. The children were expected to pull their weight, though. When she was twelve she was left at home one afternoon to mind the two youngest children, even though she was very ill with scarlet fever.

Phil remembers the harsh discipline, describing how Neville used to beat the devil out of the boys with a rubber hose. Gloria their mother was gentle, however, and they all adored her. Phil didn't mind it when she disciplined him. She'd take him into her room: 'Philip, do you know what you've done wrong?' Then it would be one belt across the bum with the wooden spoon and it was over. She never chastised him in anger, unlike his father who would belt him whether he'd erred or not. Gloria didn't raise her voice, despite the chaos of having so many children and a husband who would bring home several visitors at a time, always unannounced, and always in time for the family meal. She was extremely quiet, never overbearing: the perfect, meek woman.

Phil describes her as an amazing mother. She read to her children every night, and sang to them. When they did wrong, she was decisive with their punishments, then gave them a hug. All her children knew that she loved and adored them.

Money was tight and often Gloria had to make a little food go a long way. Phil recalls the tasty soups she made from practically nothing. If Neville arrived home with five or so visitors, Gloria never complained – she just added more water and a few more vegetables to the soup pot. To Phil's mind it was a magic pot that fed everyone and never ran out.

By 1965 Neville had moved his family to Cairns from where he conducted tent campaigns throughout northern Queensland, taking his vision of a God-centred society to people in remote areas. Gloria benefited from the move because her mother-in-law was now close enough to make regular visits. She would bring baking and sewing and would help Gloria with the housework and childcare.

Neville threw his energy in to his evangelising. Home movies made at the time, even though they have no sound track, show something of the impact he must have had on the isolated communities he preached in. Captured on film, people walk through the bush, or arrive in cattle trucks to the outback cattle station or tiny community where Neville has set up his base. He pilots his own plane, bringing with him helpers and the big marquee with its large banner reading, VOICE OF DELIVERANCE EVANGELISTIC CAMP. Smaller tents are set up near the marquee – possibly accommodation for Neville and his helpers. The plane, too, has VOICE OF DELIVERANCE painted boldly on the fuselage. The people come dressed for the occasion despite the tropical climate. The women, Aboriginal and European, mostly wear Sunday-best hats; the men are tidily dressed, some in suits, most at least wearing a tie with a white shirt. Shots of the congregation show them singing, clapping, and waving their arms in the air. The full immersion baptisms take place in streams nearby.

Footage taken at Port Douglas shows Neville's plane where it has landed on the beach. Cars in which the congregation have arrived line the grass at the edge of the sand. The whole Cooper family runs hand in hand down the beach towards the camera: Neville, Gloria and all their blond-headed children in a row from tallest to shortest. This is a high day, a holiday – a holy day, with a service on the beach followed by baptism in the ocean of the converts who all wear white.

Neville's reputation as a vital and dynamic preacher over-shadowed any dissension, and the invitations to speak kept flooding in. In 1967 he accepted another request from New Zealand to give a speaking tour, and decided to take the whole family, possibly with the idea that he would live there permanently. Gloria packed up the nine children they had by then, including her new baby, named Miracle by Neville in thanks for his survival when he crashed his plane in the outback. It had taken searchers several days to find him and this sixth daughter was born shortly afterwards.

It was winter when he drove his family out of Cairns, heading for Sydney where they would board the ship for New Zealand. Neville heated bricks to keep the children warm during the long car trip.

Phil was five when the family arrived in New Zealand but he remembers the planes towing the banners across the sky: HEAR NEVILLE COOPER TONIGHT. His father was big news, drawing crowds comparable to those who flocked to hear the American evangelist Billy Graham. People responded to Neville's charisma as much as to his message. He preached of a new utopia where the individual sacrificed his will to God, where people gave up the selfish life and lived instead for the glory of God, where they put others before self, and God above all.

While he was on tour, Neville settled his family in the small North Island town of Feilding. It was there that Stephen, the child born between Phil and Miracle, contracted diphtheria and died. He was five years old.

After a year in Feilding, Neville moved his family to the Canterbury town of Rangiora where he continued to preach, collecting followers who were attracted to the idea of living a Godly life and who saw him as somebody they could trust, who had knowledge and wisdom and would lead them in this new way. Decades later, Faith still meets people whose lives her father transformed through his preaching. They speak of him with awe and gratitude for the way he turned their lives around. They speak of him with love.

In Rangiora, the family joined the City New Life Church. Neville easily found work to fit in with his evangelising and, as always, was an energetic and hard worker for whom earning money was secondary to his driving vision of creating a Christian utopia.

Life went on much as before for Gloria, except that now she didn't have the help of her mother-in-law. In the years from 1968 to 1971 she had four more babies: Michael, David, Daniel and Christian.

True to form, Neville fell out with the pastor of City New Life and in 1969 broke away. This time, instead of moving his family away from Rangiora, he gathered his followers to him, and continued to preach his vision of life according to the word of God. Without a base from which to preach, he simply hired the local St Johns Ambulance Hall down the road from the City New Life Church. Lack of a proper venue didn't put people off and he continued to draw followers from all over the country, with many settling in Rangiora or its environs in order to attend his services and take part in the ministry he ran, helping those less fortunate.

Naomi and Judah Benjamin came with their children, joining Neville's ministry in 1974, when their oldest daughter Sandra was 16. They were recent converts to Christianity and had left army careers in Australia to attend the Faith Bible College in Tauranga. They were looking for a place where people lived according to the word of God, and Neville's Christian philosophy of working together for the good of all seemed to be exactly what they'd been searching for.

Phil, then 12 years old, was intrigued by the bubbly teenaged Sandy. She was a Christian, but not like those he was used to. He saw that she had a bit of attitude – not rebellious or in any way disobedient. It was more to do with the mystique of the outside world, symbolised to him by her hippy-style leather bag with *Jesus Loves Me* carved into it. Neville banned the bag – it was too worldly – and Sandra gave it up willingly. To Phil, she had an exotic edge. She was out-going, laughed easily, and he would hear her singing as she went about her work. She was a friendly, open young woman who loved kids and he'd often see her comforting a crying toddler or playing with a group of little ones. Phil found it slightly puzzling that this girl fitted in so easily to the group of his father's followers when she'd come from the world where she'd been free to be whatever she wanted. She was a talented swimmer and could have gone on to compete internationally, maybe even at the Olympics – but instead she had chosen to live an austere life of service to others for the love of God.

The Benjamins joined the group at a time when Neville's followers were by-and-large respected and admired in the local community. They were easily recognisable by their modest dress: mid-calf-length dresses for the women and sober garb for the men. The Cooperites, as they became known, would gather together to work for the good of others, doing up old cars to give away, helping establish gardens, and extending help and fellowship to those in need. The local mayor spoke of them as a tremendous asset to the district. Naomi and Judah, along with hundreds of others, found in Neville's community a wonderful example of true Christian living.

Phil's eldest sister, Faith, married her teacher husband Alan in 1970. The young couple settled on his parents' small farm at Springbank, between Rangiora and the small township of Cust, purchasing the property from Alan's parents soon afterwards when they wanted to retire. The young couple were happy to agree to Neville's proposal of establishing a religious school on their property, where parents could be confident their children were being taught sound moral values. The school at Springbank, one of the first religious schools to be set up in New Zealand, started off with 12 pupils but quickly grew. Demand was so great that a secondary department was soon set up, staffed by teachers from among Neville's followers.

Life became more curtailed for Phil in 1976 when his father decided to move his family from Rangiora to Springbank, to live in the big old farmhouse recently vacated by Faith and Alan who had built a new house on the property. Faith looked forward to having her mother and the rest of the family living closer to her, but for 13-year-old Phil, there would be even less freedom than he'd had in town because it was impossible to go anywhere without his father's permission.

The Cooperites were highly visible in the small community and admiration of them was not universal. As they became more closed off from the world, workers who went into people's homes used the opportunity to preach their leader's gospel. They'd criticise wives for not being submissive, husbands for not being head of the household, and both of them for the way they raised their children.

Judith Graham who lived with her husband Reg in Cust at the time remembers the Cooperites being viewed with suspicion by some. Neville would evangelise to recruit people on the weekends, targeting unsophisticated people who would trust him, projecting himself as a father figure who would provide shelter and security.

Judith's own contact with the Cooperites didn't encourage her to view them positively. She and Reg contracted two of the men to install a wood stove, with the work to be done in their absence. The workmanship was excellent and they were pleased with the result. Then Neville rang Reg to ask if he could borrow their television. Reg wasn't happy about the request and said so, whereupon Neville snapped, 'Why not? You've got two.'

The second set was upstairs where the workmen had had no call to go.

On another occasion, some of their tradesmen came to ask if they could look at the renovations the Grahams had had done on the house. When they came to the master bedroom, one of the Cooperite men made an inappropriate remark which shocked Judith and she left the room. Reg quickly showed the men the door.

Judith also remembers one of the sons running away.

It would have been Phil. He hated the lifestyle his father imposed on him and his siblings. It seemed to him that Neville always had time for others but not for his own children who had to work at his community projects whether they wanted to or not. His father was proud of his large family and always included a photo of them in his pamphlets, something Phil found hypocritical even then. The incident at Queenstown was always in his mind and he couldn't understand how a father who was proud of his children could threaten to disown his son.

In 1976, a couple of months before his fourteenth birthday, he ran away from home, walking out to the main road where he hitchhiked north.

At Kaikoura a priest picked him up, was concerned for the welfare of his young passenger, and invited him home to have dinner and stay the night. Phil was starving and glad of the hot meal. The priest showed him to the spare room where he'd made up the bed. Phil's lucky day: food, bed and board. Running away from home was a piece of cake, or so it seemed until the priest came into the bathroom while Phil was in the shower. Later he came and sat on Phil's bed. Phil didn't grasp the possible implications, but he was scared. Once the man left the room, Phil crept from the house and ran. He walked around the town all that night, too frightened to sleep.

After the longest night of his life, home didn't look so bad and he went back. The upshot of his burst of rebellion, though, was unexpected: Neville decided his son needed a change of scene and took him and Gloria to Australia for a holiday. They stayed in Coffs Harbour north of Sydney with a friend, a man Neville had converted during one of his campaigns. He'd been a reluctant convert, punching Neville to the ground the first time he went to a meeting, but he had come back for more.

Coffs Harbour made a big impression on Phil; he loved the sea and he loved being able to run on the beach whenever he wanted to. The Cooper children rarely went far beyond their Springbank home and so he'd had little experience of the seaside. When the holiday was over he returned to school and to being a disaffected student.

During this period Neville was still travelling each Sunday to the hall in Rangiora to preach. He continued evangelising with the result that more and more people were drawn to him, with some like Naomi and Judah Benjamin moving to the Springbank property to live near their leader. The atmosphere was one of cooperation, where members worked together and supported each other, all with the purpose of living according to God's word. They held Christmas camps during the summer break when all Neville's followers would pitch tents or set up caravans on the farm at Springbank for the two week duration.

Phil found the lack of personal freedom and Neville's insistence that the family join the community working bees increasingly stifling. He found school boring and he was glad to leave the moment he turned 15 in 1977, to work for the builder Neville apprenticed him to. Phil enjoyed the work but, even better, earning money of his own. With money, he could escape from the community and his father. He would go far away where he could be free of his father's control, free to live as he pleased. He saved his pay until he had enough money to book a plane ticket to Brisbane. While he saved, he studied the road code because sitting his driver's licence would give him the excuse he needed to go into Rangiora. From there he would make his escape to Christchurch Airport.

On the appointed day he shoved his passport and ticket into his jacket pocket and went off to Rangiora to sit the licence, passing easily because he'd been driving machinery since he was a kid. Coming back in from the driving test, he glanced into the office and saw his father waiting for him.

Phil didn't know how Neville had found out he didn't intend coming home, but he didn't hang about to ask. He was determined to escape, to get away from his father's rules, and to find out if the outside world was as wicked and evil as his dad preached that it was. He took off around the back of the building. A taxi! He flagged it down and asked how much the fare would be to Christchurch Airport. Thirty dollars? Good, he had fifty.

It was a nerve-wracking ride. He was sure Neville would follow him but he didn't want to make the cabbie suspicious by turning around and staring out the rear window.

There was no sign of Neville at the airport. Phil boarded the plane with no luggage and just 20 dollars to his name. Would his father come storming down the aisle of the plane, demanding that he get off? Phil sat tense and watchful until the plane lifted off the runway.

When he got to Brisbane, he hitchhiked out of the city, getting a ride from two Mormons who took him in and helped him find work. While he was living with them he converted to their faith, even though he knew Neville would have disowned him for embracing what he considered a false religion. Phil, though, was prepared to do whatever it took to survive on the outside. The question of whether to believe his father's religion or that of the Mormons didn't worry him too much. Death was a long way off and meanwhile there was a whole new world to experience. He bought forbidden things with the money he earned, and delighted in their ownership: a digital watch, a tape recorder and worldly music tapes that he listened to with enjoyment made greater by knowing that his father would disapprove. The freedom of being able to do exactly as he pleased was heady – he could turn on the radio, go to the movies, go to the beach whenever he had time off work, and swim in the sea. But all the time, he felt the overpowering loss of his family.

Back in New Zealand, Neville hadn't forgotten his son, and set in motion enquiries that would eventually discover his whereabouts, but in the interim he was busy, working at various jobs to support his family, and preaching. Although his followers also contributed money to help with expenses, Neville was never interested in accumulating money for his personal aggrandisement. He was a true man of God: moral, upright and unflinchingly honest. But gradually his vision of a religious utopia was changing as he became convinced that communal living was essential if people were to worship God with the whole of their hearts and minds. When young couples married, he encouraged them to live near him on the Springbank property. This was a major step and signalled the beginning of the complete separation from the outside world that would come in just a few years. His followers embraced the idea of community life and made financial sacrifices to enable the dream to come to fruition. Men with trades continued to work on the outside, with their pay going towards the building project. Women stopped shopping for all but the most essential items – those that couldn't be made or grown on site. Possibly some of the members sold property and donated the proceeds because, in accordance with his beliefs, Neville didn't approach any institution for a loan for the proposed building. The men also contributed their labour, which often meant working on the community buildings during the weekends and evenings. Life was hard, but working for a common goal created a climate of loving cooperation. There was a sense that they were building a Christian island in a Godless world. The women particularly loved the companionship and valued the strong friendships they formed.

Neville designed the accommodation blocks so that each family had two small bedrooms and shared a lounge and bathroom with two or three adjoining families. There were segregated dormitories for young unmarried men and women, along with single rooms for newly married couples or older couples whose children had their own families.

The only kitchen was large and – as money allowed – well-equipped, so that the women could provide meals for the whole community. There was a single large laundry capable of handling all the personal items as well as sheets, towels and work clothes.

The face of Springbank changed. Neville and his family

continued to live in the original farmhouse, and Faith and Alan in their new home. However, locals travelling along the road could now see the two large accommodation blocks, as well.

Lack of money pressed the community to become as self-sufficient as possible, and during the Springbank years they produced all their own food, even growing and milling their own flour. The farm was small, but supported a piggery and about 15 cows which kept the whole community in milk, cheese and butter.

The men built the first methane gas converter used in New Zealand, converting cow, pig and chicken manure from neighbouring farms into methane gas, with which they ran all their vehicles. The community's increasing self-sufficiency reduced the opportunities for worldly contact, as did the fact that gradually members gave up their paid jobs to work inside the community. Money was tight, but everyone was in the same situation and cohesiveness came from supporting each other and working together for the common good.

Phil was in Coffs Harbour during the transition, when some families were in accommodation blocks at Springbank, and others in their own homes in Rangiora or the surrounding towns. Ironically, Neville was preaching equality and freedom of choice, but not dispensing them. Often, it was just small things, such as those living on site being able to get their washing in if it rained during Saturday working bees, while those who lived outside could not, and they'd get upset about the unfairness of it. The working bees had changed, too. Whereas they used to be voluntary half-day sessions, they were now compulsory all-day affairs, and if you didn't turn up, somebody would be coming and knocking on your door to ask why.

As more of them began living at Springbank itself Neville's increasing control over his followers disturbed more people than just his wayward son. Disquiet was growing as Neville moved closer to his ideal of having all his followers on site, and people began leaving his flock as more rules were introduced and his control tightened.

CHAPTER TWO:
THE EVOLUTION TO COMMUNITY

To be a friend of the world is to be an enemy of God,
for friendship with the world is enmity with God.
What We Believe, p. 35

A change that caused many to break away from Neville was his expectation that his followers espouse the concept of what he called the sharing life. Those who were employed would pool their money to support others in the community. Those who were rich in possessions would sell them and give the money to those in need. He cited the apostles who gave up all they had, claiming ownership of nothing so that all possessions were held in common to be used for the good of all. This, Neville believed, would create a true Christian community where nobody wanted for anything and all were cared for equally. Faith and Alan felt that the principle was good, but that people should only give up their possessions if they chose to; it should never be something that they were forced to do.

In 1977, eight years after he broke away from City New Life in Rangiora, Neville Cooper formally set up his own church, calling it the Christian Church at Springbank. He introduced more rules, setting out how people must dress, how they must worship, the roles of men and women, and how parents should raise their children. He stipulated that women must always dress modestly in long skirts, sleeves to the wrist and without flesh visible on the chest. They must not cut their hair, which was to be worn loose and hanging down the back. Headscarves would be worn. Men, when they weren't working, would wear long-sleeved shirts, ties, and dark trousers. Children, too, must be dressed modestly. Make-up and jewellery were forbidden.

The realm of women was the home and family, therefore young, unmarried women were not to work in the outside world. There was plenty for them to do helping their married sisters. Young men would be apprenticed appropriately and Neville would decide on the trade each would follow. Early marriages were encouraged because, according to Neville, only through marriage could young people manage their God-given sexual urges. He set up protocols about marriage, one being that couples had to get his permission to marry. One of his sons asked permission to marry Sandra Benjamin – Neville refused and ordered him to marry another young woman. He obeyed his father – it was either that or leave and be cast out and cut off from his family forever.

Neville instituted timetables and rosters. Meals were always at the same times: breakfast at 6.30, lunch at 12.30 and dinner at 6 p.m. He organised the work on a roster system so that the tasks such as milking, laundry, childcare, cooking and dish-washing were shared around. Each meal began with a grace and Neville would read from a book or newspaper to his assembled people while they ate. Life wasn't all work – each weekend there was a young people's night of singing, dancing, and sometimes a video approved by Neville. After church on Sundays members would gather to watch the young men play soccer.

For some, the regimentation and rules, along with the requirement to sell up everything they owned, was too much, and people continued to leave, but others stayed, believing that their leader was preparing them for eternal life.

In 1978, as Neville began drawing the year-old church further apart from the outside world, Alan decided he wanted to leave Springbank with all its rules and prohibitions, but Faith wouldn't go. To leave would mean breaking from her family because she knew her father would disown her and forbid any contact with her siblings or her mother. It was difficult, too, to contemplate life outside the community at Springbank. Alan taught in its school and all their friends were members. It was a good life filled with friendship, where the details of daily living were taken care of: you had no money worries; you always had food and shelter. Your life had purpose as you helped others and worshipped God.

But they could see that Neville was tightening his control over his people.

Judah Benjamin also began to get twitchy. He feared that Neville was becoming like some of the infamous cult leaders who had wrought such devastation on their followers. He asked his wife Naomi, 'Do you reckon this outfit is getting like Jim Jones's?' He worried that Neville's utter belief that his was the right way, the only way, was leading to trouble. He saw the gradual erosion of basic principles such as equality for all and personal modesty. But, like Faith, Naomi didn't want to leave. On many levels life was good and she knew that if she left, her children would choose not to go with her and that she'd never see them again.

It was becoming clear that Neville felt he was invincible. He saw himself as called and chosen by Jesus. He believed that the leader should have others to help him make decisions, but that always his would be the ultimate authority. In the hierarchy of this 'equal' society, men had authority over women, whose headscarves symbolised their submission. Although they were allowed to read the scripture, women were not permitted to teach the gospel or to preach. Naomi fell foul of that rule when she expounded one day on a scripture she'd read. Neville rebuked her for usurping the role given to men. 'If I said anything, or if a woman said anything, you were told to mind your own business, or to stop being a sticky beak and to get your nose out of it.' A woman was quickly slapped down for any show of independence.

Men were also subjected to their leader's control if they questioned a decision, as Alan did over the gardens. He was a good gardener and a generous one, giving surplus produce to others. But when Neville decided that the gardens would be made communal, gardening became a duty and it killed the joy of it for Alan. He told Neville this and as a result was summoned to a men's meeting. (*Those who sin before all, should be rebuked before all, that others may learn to fear.* WHAT WE BELIEVE, P. 55)

The men's meetings go on until the miscreant repents. Sometimes they will continue all night, with the men repeating the same messages: Why have you got such a selfish heart? Why are you so rebellious?

Alan's protests that they were missing the point cut no ice. He was in error and he was the one who must submit. He did so because there was no alternative other than to leave the community.

It was partly this increasing control that Phil had run to Australia to escape, but he missed his family and when the feeling of loss became unbearable he went looking for somebody with a connection to home. Colin and Dawn who had become family friends after Neville's conversion of Colin, welcomed him into their home and gave him work on their cane farm and tropical fruit orchard north of Cairns.

Eventually Neville discovered Phil's whereabouts. He sent his daughter Charity to persuade her brother to come home, knowing that Phil would feel greater emotional pressure from his sister than he would from one of the men. This was an example of the kind of inequality that Faith and Alan had objected to: perks such as travel were given to Coopers and Charity was a Cooper. But Neville would also have chosen her because she knew what to say, how to work on his guilt: *Your family misses you; Mum's very upset; how can you do this to her?*

Phil refused to return. He'd left because he was sick of being caged and unable to go freely beyond the confines of the property at Springbank; he didn't want to be harnessed and he wanted to experience the world. However he was still very young and Charity's visit had the desired effect. Seeing her again intensified his longing for his family so that when Neville sent two of the men over to bring him back, he decided to go with them of his own free will.

Once Phil was home, Neville welcomed him. He was an obedient son again and was allowed to resume his apprenticeship.

However it wasn't long before he was subjected to the discipline system. His boss belonged to the church and he didn't like it that Phil had come back with a bit of an attitude – that he wore a worldly watch, and now owned a tape recorder and listened to worldly music on it. He called a men's meeting. At one p.m. Phil had to turn up at the old farmhouse where Neville and his family still lived, go into Neville's room and sit on the bed. All adult men of the community were there, as Neville required them to be, about 25 or 30 of them, sitting on the floor around the room and blocking the door. They tried to get Phil to talk, but he wouldn't say anything. It went on for hours. *What's the problem? Why are you so worldly? There is sin in your life. You must submit to your elders. God's going to judge you.* On and on. The men dissected every aspect of his behaviour, asking him why he'd said this or that, why he was so disrespectful, how he could shame his family like this; couldn't he see he was breaking his mother's heart?

Phil sat there, refusing to react to anything. Neville demanded that he change his name. 'I don't want to be associated with you. Change your name.'

While Phil recognised the bombardment as another of his father's mind games, he shrugged it off, but made a silent vow: he would never change his name. If his father wanted to disassociate from his son then let him change his own name.

After three hours of hounding, Phil experienced another defining moment, similar in impact to the incident at Queenstown. Neville said, 'Philip, pass me your watch.' Phil handed over his pride and joy – the digital watch he'd bought in Australia.

Neville took it, looked his son in the eye, then smashed the watch down on the edge of the table. It shattered and he threw it to the floor. Neither worldly objects nor disobedience would be tolerated at Springbank.

Phil got up and went to the door, walking past the men who all stood up. He walked downstairs to his bedroom and began packing. He was very focused; there was no emotion. But Neville hadn't finished. He knew how much Phil adored his mother so he piled on the pressure by sending in Gloria and one of his sisters. Gloria was in tears. His sister kept asking, 'What are you doing? You can't do this.'

He hated making his mother cry, and he hated upsetting his sister but he was still determined to leave. At about seven o'clock Neville came in with the men. His message was brief: 'You are no longer my son. I wish you'd never been born.'

Phil ignored him.

But still Neville didn't give up. Somehow he would get a reaction. He couldn't use his usual argument that the outside world was nothing but evil and wickedness because Phil had just come from there, so he chose another threat: if Phil were to leave that night something terrible might happen to him because God was going to take him down the road and judge him. Phil could have a major accident and die, or he could end up crippled for life and then what would happen to him with no family to care for him? What would he do, crippled in the outside world where nobody cared whether he lived or died? People outside were selfish, they'd rob him of anything he had and how could he protect himself if he was injured? Phil must realise that God had no love for the selfish of heart, for those who went against his wishes.

The threats of what could happen were graphic, detailed and relentless. It was a well-polished script, and Neville's delivery of it was forceful and full of dramatic intensity.

At about eight o'clock, completely exhausted, Phil cracked. He took the worldly tape recorder, and threw it to the floor where it smashed. That action broke the deadlock. Neville had finally achieved his aim. His father hugged him, this obedient son whom he loved again. Phil was 16 years old.

Similar unfair and psychologically damaging incidents mounted up. Faith and Alan feared for the future of the community but they couldn't change Neville's ideas. In 1979, a year after Alan had first wanted to leave, Faith realised that they couldn't stay. They had five children by this time and knew that if they wanted to keep their family intact they would have to go while the children were young. They had already seen families split when parents had left but their teenage or married children had stayed behind.

They left on a Sunday. Alan went to tell Neville they were leaving and Neville called a full men's meeting that lasted all day. Neville wanted to bring Faith in, but Alan wouldn't let him. She was grateful because Neville was her dad; she'd had a good relationship with him when she was growing up and she loved him.

But with each founding member who left, the principle they stood up for was lost. For Faith and Alan it had been important to stay connected to the outside world, and when they left there was no longer any opposition to the community isolating themselves further. That Sunday was the last time Neville held an open meeting in the hall in Rangiora, where anybody could walk in. Neville's preaching was no longer open to public scrutiny. Rules could now be introduced without the need to moderate them against outside norms.

Faith and Alan packed up their five children and left with nothing except their car, household items, and clothes. Their departure was problematic for the community, because Faith and Alan owned the land, while the community owned the accommodation blocks and some of the farm buildings. Faith and Alan were too distressed to negotiate, but they were certain about one thing: they would not walk out of Springbank with bitterness and if they had to lose financially because of their move then so be it. They would do what was right.

They left in February of 1979, and Alan immediately found relieving teaching in Rangiora. Through hard work and careful management, they have prospered in the outside world, even though they eventually forfeited most of the value of the farm at Springbank. They have also had four more children.

Neville tells his followers that when people leave the community they stop having children, they get divorced, and their lives are misery. Faith and Alan live according to Christian values but that isn't acceptable to Neville. He has disowned his daughter.

To begin with, Faith found life outside the Springbank community hard. Had it been right to leave, or was her father right, that she and her family would be damned? She drew on her childhood memories of going to church in Australia and compared the teachings she'd received there to the ones Neville preached at Springbank. The family hadn't been damned then, so why would they be now? Logically, she could see that there was no reason they'd be damned to hell for leaving, but it was a struggle to overcome the belief. Looking back, she considers that the idea of eternal salvation being possible only for those living in the Springbank community crept in with all the other changes. It wasn't espoused when they were part of City New Life. She realised that Neville, supported by a core group of men, used fear to bolster his control.

The worldly changes were less fraught to make. She and Alan took them slowly, thinking through each change until they felt it was the right thing to do. Some were easy, such as shortening hems and sleeves on their clothes. They worked through other issues such as playing sport on Sunday and women wearing trousers. They made what they would later consider mistakes, such as forbidding the children to play sport on Sunday, but they were always prepared to look at what they were doing, and to change their minds if necessary.

Going to church was the hardest. All her life, Faith had been taught to accept authority, to criticise any 'outside' teaching but not to analyse it, and now she was being exposed to ideas that turned everything upside down. What was right?

She remembers very clearly sitting in church, bowing her head and saying, 'God, I'm so confused.' The thought came into her head as an answer to a prayer: when you eat something that's good for you, like a T-bone steak, you discard the bones, and take the meat.

That was her answer: grasp hold of what was good and throw the rest away. It created a freedom in her, not just with the church but in daily life. She realised she wasn't going to agree with everyone but that she could use her own mind and intelligence to work out what she should embrace and what should be discarded.

While Faith and Alan were working out how to live in the outside world, Phil also had to find a new way of operating. He had chosen to go back to Springbank, but if he was going to stay, he saw that he wouldn't be able to continue to defy his father. He had no choice but to conform and, just as he dealt with everything in his life, he did it wholeheartedly. He worked every waking hour to become the ideal son, the apple of his father's eye, the heir apparent. It wasn't a conscious decision to give heart and soul to becoming the son his father wanted. He simply saw it as the only way to survive.

CHAPTER THREE:
MARRIAGE AND FAMILY LIFE

I will bear my own burden, do my share of the work,
and seek to bear others' burdens also.
WHAT WE BELIEVE, P. 24

After Faith and Alan's departure, Neville was able to almost totally isolate his community from the outside world. All his followers now lived on site in the purpose-built accommodation blocks in a community in which Neville's word was law and he the absolute ruler.

Phil dealt with his father's rule by keeping his head down to achieve his goal of being the hardest worker. He was the one who ran the dishwasher at community meals; he got up early to help hand-milk the 15 cows; he looked for opportunities to help anyone in need. When he heard that the doctor who served the community lived in an old house with a ramshackle kitchen, he gathered up a couple of the boys and the three of them rebuilt and refitted the kitchen at no cost to the doctor.

He went back to the community's high school to act as a role model for some of the teenage boys who were restless and struggling under Neville's rule. He was the bad guy made good, the one they could look up to. He soon discovered that getting up early to milk had an unexpected bonus. Sandra Benjamin was often rostered on cheese-making duty so that when he carried the buckets of milk to the dairy he was able to snatch a few forbidden minutes to chat to her.

Neville was still evangelising at this stage and would send vanloads of the young people into Christchurch to witness to their faith in Cathedral Square. Neville controlled the seating in the vans, lining everyone up and assigning them places. Phil soon worked out how to get his own way about who to sit with. He'd lurk out of sight, and as soon as he saw Sandy Benjamin or Erica, another girl he liked, about to board a van he'd rush up. 'Here I am, Dad.' Neville would tell him to get in.

On the 45-minute drive into Christchurch, Phil would pretend to go to sleep and Sandy would take his head and lean it against her shoulder. He had to work hard to keep the smile off his face, but he also knew that she was a motherly girl who regarded him as a kid.

He loved witnessing to the public. He was the reprobate made good and he was going to bring enlightenment to the world, telling everyone how Jesus had turned his life around. He was charged up and full of adrenalin for the mighty task before him. Often he got heckled. One day he answered back, shouting out to a man, 'And you're just like your father, the devil!'

The man flattened him with a punch that broke his nose. Phil went home that night feeling heroic. He'd taken a punch for Jesus; he was a martyr who had spilt his blood for the cause.

It wasn't the only time he broke his nose. He loved Sundays because of the afternoon soccer games. He was the most competitive player. A friendly match where the outcome didn't matter wasn't his style. He went into each game determined to win. He got into arguments over his play and had to show up at many men's meetings where his aggressive competitiveness was deplored. It's only a game, they told him. He didn't care, just as he didn't care about his injuries. The game where his nose ended up squashed sideways across his face was a highlight because the community asked Sandy to take him to the hospital in Christchurch to get it fixed. He felt no pain at all during the journey.

He got involved with every aspect of community life, dreaming up new ideas and making them happen. He and his older brother Mark decided to put on a special dinner for the married couples. The meal was elaborate, as were the decorations which included a model plane they built as the centrepiece of the dining hall.

Neville had broken him and Phil's response was to remake himself in his father's image. He was so successful that after only a year he was considered the perfect son. Neville spoke of him to others with pride, and began to give him increasing responsibility. The prodigal had returned.

Soon after his eighteenth birthday in 1980, Sandy Benjamin filled Phil's thoughts and dreams more than ever, but the rules prohibited young people spending time alone together until Neville gave them permission to do so, although Phil became adept at finding opportunities. The young couple were virgins and their naïvely innocent courtship led to a problem for Phil in that his testicles became tight and sore. He went to his father to talk to him about Sandy and to ask if Neville would give him permission to court her. Neville questioned him: Why did he think Sandy was the woman he wanted to marry and how long had he thought so? He asked Phil how he felt about the prospect of marriage, which gave Phil the opportunity to mutter that his testicles were sore and he was worried about it.

Neville was reassuring, telling him that it wasn't unusual and wouldn't be a problem once he was married. He asked Phil to show him. Phil complied, but was utterly shocked when his father masturbated him.

In hindsight he can see what should have happened: 'He should have told me to do it myself. I've got two hands and it wasn't as if I didn't know how. I think he did it to some of my brothers, too, but they won't talk about it, or they can't. I knew I should have stopped it, but part of me was thinking, *This is my dad, my leader.* Instead, I shut it out – pretended it hadn't happened.'

He knew there was no excuse for what his father did, but he also knew that the price of objecting was the withdrawal of his father's love and of losing Sandy as well, because his father would never give permission to one who challenged him. And how could Phil object? This was the man everyone looked up to, the one God spoke through. The only thing to do was to shut out what Neville had done to him and keep quiet about it.

Two weeks after the incident, Phil asked his dad if he could marry Sandy. Neville consented to talk to Sandy on Phil's behalf, and after doing so gave his son permission to ask her, even though he'd refused to let another son marry her. Phil believes now that his father gave him permission because he knew Phil couldn't be contained and suspected he'd run away again if he refused to give his consent. Phil had always been the son who got into the most trouble and received the most beatings. Neville knew exactly how far he could push him.

Phil was 18 and a half and Sandy was 21. She refused him, telling both Neville and her own father, 'He's got to grow up yet.' But she also told Phil to ask her again in six months. He couldn't wait that long, asking her again in four months. They were married according to the law in New Zealand in 1981 a few days after Phil's nineteenth birthday. Currently in the community, couples do not marry under the law, but are married by the church in the sight of God. They make a public pledge to each other, then go to a specially prepared room to consummate the union. This done, they come out to celebrate with the community which now considers them to be a married couple.

The newly weds were given a single room in one of the dormitories to begin their life together. Phil's determination to be the hardest worker, and the best community member, didn't diminish with his marriage. Sandy loved the energy he created and was proud of his involvement in community life. She also worked hard, getting up early to work in the dairy and volunteering to do extra duties wherever she saw the need. As a couple they were esteemed for their diligence and generosity.

Phil became the woodwork teacher at the school, working with boys who were often just as restless as he had been. He became their mentor and their role model, organising them into an after-school work group, making wooden toys to sell and ploughing the money back into the school. Neville was pleased on two counts: firstly, Phil was solving the problem of how to keep the boys in line, and secondly, he was generating much-needed cash for the school.

Waterbeds had just come onto the market and when Phil heard about this new type of bed he examined one in detail. He saw that they would be easy to make and would bring in more money than the toys had been making. The first few sold quickly, and the whole enterprise just took off. Within six months it grew from a school project into the community business. Neville would say, 'Can you take this any further, Phil?' So Phil did, and had everyone in the community working for him. His father would come to him and ask, 'How many beds do we need to get out today, Phil?'

Phil was the apple of his father's eye. It was a turning point for him; at last he was in control of something and it gave him a freedom he'd never had. Neville saw the ability in him and played on it, but even that didn't detract from Phil's sense of independence over at least one area of his life.

Neville controlled everything else, including Phil's marriage. Some months after the wedding he invited the young couple to share a nice meal with him and Gloria in their room in the farmhouse. Phil and Sandy had heard from other young couples what such an invitation meant: Neville would undress the wife while the husband had to lie on the bed with Gloria. The only comfort was in knowing that he didn't actually have intercourse with the young woman. Phil and Sandy couldn't refuse: Neville was the father and the leader, which put huge psychological pressure on them to obey his commands. Phil felt utterly powerless to protect his young wife: 'Your father undresses your wife. What woman could handle that? I'm lying there and I just want to get up and walk out. My dad well and truly violated my wife – he robbed her of her dignity way back then. He had his hands all over her body; he owned her. I just wanted it to be over. I'd ask myself, is this a nightmare? Please just let it be over.'

Each time the invitation came, they would try to think of excuses but knew they had no choice. Phil would kill himself inside because that was the only way he could deal with it: don't think, don't feel any emotion, just endure till it finishes. It was a reprise of the masturbation incident and Phil dealt with it in the same manner, by shutting it away and not thinking about it. He didn't know what Sandy thought about it because the couple never discussed it. They would just glance at each other, a signal to say, *let's get out of here as soon as possible.* Such incidents occurred eight or ten times, then stopped, perhaps because Sandy's body changed as a result of child-bearing, or because Phil got so busy that he was never around. Gradually, he and Sandy had slipped out of his father's inner circle.

Such violations were part of Neville's campaign to make young couples less uptight about sex, but for Phil, there was no justification for them. As far as he was concerned, it was rape of the mind. Others who have left say that Neville breaks down the marriage relationship; he usurps the husband's role. It appears that for Neville it was something of a crusade to make sex a natural part of life rather than have it hidden and furtive. Apparently he set himself up as the authority on sexual fulfilment and saw it as his duty to bring sexual enlightenment to his followers. He believed that sexuality should be discussed openly and freely, and was nothing to be ashamed of.

Looking back now, Phil can see the damage his father inflicted. 'That's why it's about me and Dad – more than most people will realise. If that hadn't happened to Sandy, she'd still be with me today. It broke her spirit. Dad took the husband's role out of my hands. He got off on that and then had sex with Mum. She had to be there the whole time. He used my life as a tool – maybe he was struggling sexually. I'm sure he watched porn. Sometimes the door to the TV room would be shut and locked.'

Neville had always been a powerful figure, but in Phil's early childhood, he had been a model of propriety in terms of personal modesty. The children never saw either of their parents naked, even to the extent of Gloria always turning away when she was breastfeeding. Things changed radically; Neville justified what he was doing sexually and came to believe that it was right. It was cumulative, starting with couples coming to him with their problems. If doctors advised on sex problems, then Neville felt he had the right to do the same because he was the spiritual leader. He didn't actively encourage couples to come to him with sexual problems but gradually his 'counselling' got more extreme as it appeared he convinced himself that each step he took was right.

It evolved over a year to the stage where he'd get couples into the big room; they'd put blankets on the floor and each couple had to make love. There were objections and he'd back off, but he'd slowly convince himself and those around him that it was the right thing to do. At some point Neville's possibly genuine desire to help couples struggling with their sexual relationship tipped over to become an exercise in self-gratification that went unchallenged by those who could have intervened.

The conflict between his demands for absolute modesty of dress, and the immodesty of his behaviour, didn't seem to occur to him. The teenage girls were 'invited' to join Neville and some of the men in the spa pool, with everybody naked and a pornographic movie projected onto the wall. It was an invitation the girls dreaded. Again, those closest to Neville who could have stopped it chose not to.

Her husband's sexual activities must have seared Gloria to her soul. But Neville had married her when she was 16 and, in Phil's words, turned her into a baby factory. Her husband claimed to have taught her everything she knew and her only fault in the eyes of her children was that she never stood up to him. One of her grandchildren remembers her as a very quiet person who always looked sad. She was a figurehead with no power, who sat beside her husband every mealtime and nodded mutely when he'd turn to her saying, 'Isn't that so, Gloria?'

The sexualised environment Neville created was a major factor in causing people to leave, and outside the community Faith was picking up the pieces of lives broken by Neville. She believes her father has to be held accountable for his actions, as do those elders who, if they'd held their ground, would have had the power to stop him but chose instead to support his activities.

Judah Benjamin, Sandy's father, left in 1983 with his 18-year-old daughter Yvette. In a documentary made shortly before his death, he speaks from his hospital room of Neville being a devil incarnate. Judah freely admits to joining in the spa pool sessions, and to participating in the occasions when couples went to the big room and made love under their blankets. Pornography was available to any of the men who wanted it. Judah can't believe, looking back, that he was part of all that. Although he still believed in the values of modesty and Christian respect for others, he got to the point where he accepted as normal the sexual activities of the community, although he drew the line at watching porn. He doesn't explain what finally led him to walk away with nothing, leaving behind his wife, three other children, and his grandchildren. It could have been in order to support Yvette whose own suffering at Neville's hands had been harrowing.

Her husband's determined departure broke Naomi's heart. She wasn't aware at the time of the severe abuse Yvette had suffered because her daughter had been forbidden by Neville to speak of it. She did know that when Judah left, she wouldn't be allowed to see him or speak to him again. Those were the rules. It was a choice between staying and remaining part of her family still in the community, or leaving and losing them forever. She would stay.

Faith and Alan had left because they couldn't change what was happening, and to stay would have been to condone it. Faith was horrified by the way the young ones leaving the community spoke about sex. Their talk was frank and extremely crude, making them targets for trouble if they got in with the wrong crowd.

Phil didn't see leaving as an option, so he dealt with it all by immersing himself in work. The dinners he and his brother Mark put on gradually evolved, with the productions that were part of the dining experience becoming more and more elaborate. Phil masterminded and produced each event. For him, these concerts became the happiest times of his early years. He loved the whole experience, which was a great release from the monotonous daily life of the community. Those working on the productions were allowed to take a week off to concentrate on them, and Phil would work till two in the morning, going over every detail, coordinating everything, training his helpers, and making sure the whole thing would be perfect.

He involved Sandy in every concert, putting her right in the front for the singing and pushing her into the limelight. She thrived on the excitement and the opportunity to bring pleasure to others through the performance. Bringing happiness to others was much more important to her than being noticed. The selflessness of her personality was very attractive to Phil.

The hierarchy sanctioned the concerts, even allowing Phil to buy make-up and fabric for costumes. He developed a costume room in a community where the women always wore long blue dresses and the men blue shirts and black trousers. For the younger members, this was the only chance they would ever have to dress up, to be someone different.

But every show led to run-ins with Neville. Phil remembers

one incident vividly: 'I was production manager, did the lighting, controlled the shots. Dad's sitting there watching a rehearsal, up the front: "Turn the lights up. It's too dark."

'Nothing happened. I'm like, *I'm running this show.*

'He walks up the back. "I said turn the lights up. It's too dark."

'I said, "Dad, it's a production."

'He goes, "I said, turn the lights up."

'Next minute there were four or five of the men there: "Come out the back."

'So I walked back and turned all the lights up full and said, "There you are."

'I was over it. I was creating the mood and all he wanted to do was control it. For me, I lived it – I was involved in it. But for him it was just, "Can't see."'

Phil felt true to himself while he was working on the productions. This was who he was, what he loved doing. It was the excitement of leading a team, of having things always happening, and of learning to manage it all.

CHAPTER FOUR:
JUGGLING FAMILY AND BUSINESS

*Believing in something is an act of will, and the things
you believe will determine the way you act.*
LIFE IN COMMON: THE EXPERIENCE OF THE
GLORIAVALE CHRISTIAN COMMUNITY P. 4
(the community's pamphlet for visitors)

Neville might have allowed Phil limited freedom over the productions, but in all other aspects of life his control was tightening. He now required parents to give their children religiously appropriate names, or those that expressed virtues, values, or that would inspire them. Phil and Sandy's first child was born in February 1982 when Phil was just 19, and he felt the potency of having fathered a son. He adored the baby and named him Israel, not, as Neville thought, because of the biblical reference, but for a cartoon character he'd liked when he was living in Australia. Sandy had begun to fulfil her destiny as the mother of future community members and her baby received all the loving motherliness of her character. Each in their own way, she and Phil loved being parents. For Sandy, a child was the greatest gift God could bestow on her, while Phil didn't credit God so much as he took pride in his own fatherhood.

On the work front, the waterbed business was so successful that Phil stopped teaching and became the business manager for the community. Life was frantically busy but at least the community organisation meant he didn't have to worry about helping Sandy with the new baby. There were plenty of women to do that and, anyway, it wasn't a man's role to help with the children or the domestic chores.

Phil had channelled his own restlessness but was able to recognise all the signs in Michael, his younger brother. Phil was Michael's boss but the two worked in harmony without any sense of one being set above the other. Phil enjoyed his brother's humour, cheerfulness, and ability to work hard, but wasn't surprised when Michael went to their father and told him he wanted to leave.

Neville didn't call a men's meeting. He simply rejected Michael immediately; called Phil, Mark and Miracle and ordered them to drive their brother to Wellington, stay there until Michael could get his passport application processed, then put him on a plane. He gave them money for a motel, the plane fare, and $100 to launch Michael in Australia. Banishment to Australia without support of any kind was the community's method of dealing with wayward teenagers at the time. Michael wasn't the first and wouldn't be the last to be put on a plane and abandoned.

The four siblings stayed together in a motel for a week, having a great time watching all the television they could. Michael got the passport and, as instructed, his siblings took him to the airport to catch a plane for Australia. Phil hoped he'd make a go of it, but he knew how hard it would be, Michael being much the same age he'd been when he ran away to Australia.

As Phil had done, Michael missed his family sorely. If Neville had allowed Gloria or his siblings to write to him, he may have been able to make a new life for himself, but as a son who had rejected his father by leaving, he was as good as dead. All contact was prohibited.

When he came home, defeated, six months later, Phil was pleased to have him back and did all he could to help his brother settle into the community. 'I did it, and you can as well,' he told him.

Phil saw that his brother continued to struggle despite his help. Although Neville accepted Michael back, this son didn't use his energy to impress his father, the way Phil had done. It took all Michael's strength simply to stay; he couldn't play the prodigal son, as well.

In 1983 Phil and Sandy's second child was born, a daughter. Again Phil skirted around his father's notion of appropriate names. He called her Dawn after their friend in northern Australia and told Neville the name referred to the dawn of the new day.

Sandy obviously enjoyed being a mother and loved her children. The family were still living in the single room but she managed to turn it into a home and screen an area off as a bedroom for the children. Phil adored Israel and Dawn, was proud of them, and slightly amazed that here he was at 21, the father of two children.

He was also proud of being the one his father depended on for the money to run the community. The buzz he got from being at the heart of things, of having projects on the go, was addictive. The travelling he had to do as the business manager widened his horizons and a bonus was that it let him escape some of the obligatory men's meetings which were called to discuss community affairs, or to discipline a miscreant, or when a young person was to be put out of the church.

Unfortunately, though, he was at home in 1984 when Michael, having decided he definitely couldn't stay, again told Neville he wanted to leave the community. This time Neville called a meeting, ordering Gloria and all Michael's siblings to attend as well as the men. Phil will never forget it. To this day the memory of it brings back the sickness he felt, the anger he experienced on his brother's behalf, the heartbreak he saw in his mother, and the overwhelming sense of his own powerlessness.

After about two hours of pressuring Michael to stay, it was clear he wasn't going to change his mind, and Neville switched tactics. 'If you want to leave and walk out that door, then you turn around now and call your mother a slut.' His reasoning was clear to Michael: if you want to leave, then you are no son of mine and therefore your mother must have gone off with another man to get pregnant with you.

Michael withstood the barrage for as long as he could, but it was relentless, the words pounding at him, drilling into his head. In the end, desperation took over. He called his mother a slut and left, but the emotional damage from that moment went on to wreck his life and he struggled to survive on the outside. Faith cared for him through long periods of severe depression, saving her brother from several suicide attempts. He would leave her house when he recovered, and live independently, but things always got bad again. Instead of going back to his sister, he would return to the community, hoping that would be the answer. But they would take him off the anti-depressants, make him stop smoking and tell him how evil Faith was. He would ring her in utter confusion and despair. Despite what the community were telling him, he knew that she was the one who cared for him and loved him. She tried to tell them to let him stay on his medication, to get him off the illegal drugs but let him have his cigarettes in the meantime. They wouldn't listen and she would have to go and pick him up. The cycle would begin again.

Phil kept his head down and kept busy.

When Sandy gave birth to their third child in 1985, Phil named her Justine. Neville agreed to her name because it was the feminine form of 'justice'. Sandy, the good and obedient wife, made no objection. Their growing family meant they needed bigger quarters and they were given a two-bedroomed apartment with a lounge shared by families in adjacent apartments.

When their third daughter was born in December 1986, Sandy told Phil that people were criticising her because her children didn't have inspiring names and she chose Tender for the new baby. It was the first time she openly chose the path set by Neville rather than obeying her husband. Phil tried to give the name greater normality by adding Joy and the baby became Tender-Joy.

During those years, Neville kept refining his ideas about what sort of community he wanted. He made extensive studies of various historical churches, including early Anabaptists such as the Amish, the Mennonites and the Hutterites. The Hutterite philosophy appealed to him the most since he saw them as the most scriptural of all the Anabaptist churches. He also admired the fact that they had a history several hundred years old and had suffered persecution before they fled from Europe to America, but through all the turmoil had held to their beliefs. They lived in community without private ownership of goods, following the teachings of Christ and his apostles, dressing modestly and caring for each other.

In 1987 Neville invited some of the elders of one of the Bruderhof Hutterite communities in the US to come to New Zealand to visit his Church at Springbank. To the outsider there appears to be little difference between the Bruderhof and other Hutterite communities, but the Bruderhof have a history of being excommunicated from the Hutterites and then reconciling. At the time they came to New Zealand, they were associated with the Hutterites.

To Neville's followers, particularly the younger ones, these men were exotic. Phil's oldest child Israel was only five, but remembers them clearly. They dressed differently, they spoke differently, they were revered; but to the children's astonishment, they were kindly. They were also men of faith and morality and, as such, disagreed strongly with a lot of Neville's teachings and abhorred the sexualised environment he had created. A system of leadership with one man at the top who was accountable to nobody went against their beliefs of governance by eldership. There is community film footage of Neville with two of the elders: the Hutterite men are holding themselves as physically aloof as they can from an ebullient Neville. Another clip shows Neville speaking about how girls are physically ready to bear children when they are 12, and boys to father children from the age of 14, thus it is healthy to promote early marriages where young people's natural urges will find sanctioned expression. The elder makes no comment. He doesn't look at Neville and his grave expression never changes.

Despite their misgivings, the elders agreed to Neville's plan of taking 30 of his young unmarried followers to America on a tour of their communities. Perhaps they hoped they could influence him to run a more Godly church, but in any case the trip went ahead.

Phil's job was to stay at home earning the money to pay for it. He was deeply disappointed at not being able to go. He handled his disappointment in the usual way, by burying himself in his work.

His home life was busy, too, with their next daughter arriving in October 1988. He called her Crystal, telling his father he'd chosen the name because it meant clear and pure. Sandy accepted it, probably because Neville did.

Life was hectic for the young couple. Sandy wholeheartedly embraced community living. It was her ideal in that she was able to be a mother as well as live a life dedicated to serving God. At least the distressing visits to Neville's room – or his to theirs, when he came to 'do something nice for your wife' which meant undressing and massaging her – had ceased. Phil tried to forget that they'd ever happened.

He was working so hard that he seldom had time to spend with Sandy and the children.

Of those years, Israel remembers his mother taking the five children everywhere she went. Tender-Joy especially was her little shadow, never letting her mother out of her sight. She was soft and gentle while the others were adventurous and boisterous, although Sandy never let any of them get out of control. Wild children would not have been tolerated, and she was too much of a loving, hands-on parent for them to need to rebel, although Justine's strong will caused her some worry.

Whenever Sandy was making bread, shelling peas, mixing scones, or doing any other suitable duty, she involved the children, singing to them and quietly showing them how to do tasks they could handle. She instilled leadership and caring into Israel and Dawn as the two eldest, but they both adored babies and were only too happy to take charge of Crystal.

When Sandy had free time, she and the children would crowd into one of their small bedrooms, sit on the beds and sing songs together. She would read to them and play games. The songs were often those from one of the few videos Neville deemed suitable for community viewing. A favourite, that the whole community saw so many times they all knew the songs by heart, was the story about the donkey that carried Mary to Jerusalem.

Phil was very much a weekend dad but whenever he was at home during the week, he'd take Israel with him into the workshop and give him simple jobs to do. Israel's favourite was taping up the pallets the waterbeds went out in, but sweeping the floor, sorting nails – everything was fun with Dad there to praise and encourage him. Sandy, though, was the centre of the children's lives. Israel remembers her motherliness, the security of knowing she would always come to soothe and comfort him when he woke in the night with a bout of the colic that plagued him, no matter what time of the night it was or how often she'd already had to get up.

Life for Phil was too stressful. The more successful the business became, the harder it was to keep it going without borrowing money, which Neville forbade him from doing. Christians, he said, did not get into debt. With no cash flow, Phil was finding it almost impossible to keep the business afloat. His businessman friend, Clive Bilbie, came to the rescue by acting as factor for the community, providing much-needed cash flow. When Phil received an order, he would invoice Clive for the amount needed to buy materials. Once the customer paid the community, money was repaid to Clive plus the interest he charged for the service.

Clive became Phil's valued friend and mentor, a situation Neville tolerated out of financial necessity, even though Clive wasn't a

Christian. A kindly father-figure, he and his wife Sue gave Phil a different perspective on family life. Theirs was a companionship between equals, of the sort not possible inside the community. Phil hadn't grown up witnessing that sort of relationship, either. His adored mother was an obedient and submissive wife who never questioned her husband's authority over her or their children. Phil had never thought about the imbalance of authority between himself and Sandy. He was the head of the household, which they both accepted, expecting him to take that role. They also knew that Phil's position as head of his own household counted for nothing in any disagreements with his father. Neville's word ruled supreme.

Clive became the role model for Phil of what a husband and father could be. In turn, Clive appreciated that Phil wanted nothing from him materially – something he found unusual because as he was well off he tended to attract people who wanted money from him. All Phil wanted was the friendship. Living in the Springbank community meant he had no need for money and in itself it held no attraction for him.

Clive wanted Phil to go with him to a waterbed show in the United States. The experience would be good for him, both in terms of the business and in letting him see something of the wider world, but Phil knew that Neville would object to the cost. Between them, Clive and Phil concocted a plan to discount an invoice to Clive for the cost of the ticket, and they told Neville that Clive would pay for it. Neville gave his permission.

The trip was another defining experience for Phil. His time in America showed him, again, that there was much more to life than the community could offer. It made him look at relationships differently, too. Clive's wife Sue had written notes for her husband

and hidden them in his luggage for him to find. Phil had never seen love expressed in such a way. Spouses in the community simply performed their set roles towards each other and towards their children. They saw no need to work at a relationship.

On his return home, nothing had changed, and the pressure from Neville was as relentless as ever. Phil continued working such long hours that he barely saw Sandy and the children, and there was no chance of enhancing his relationship with them.

Phil held himself apart from the internal politics of the community as much as he could, avoiding the men's meetings when possible. A steady trickle of people were leaving the community. Some left without telling anyone they were going, but others were open about their intentions and so were subjected to the men's meetings. No matter how a person left, once they had gone they were painted as evil. Neville and the hierarchy preached that young ones who left got into drugs, alcohol and fornication – that they ended up in jail, which two of the teenage boys would later do as a self-fulfilling prophesy. The outside world was evil, it was wicked, and the only way to eternal salvation was to stay in Neville's community at Springbank.

Although the community had its dark underside, there was also joy in practising their faith, in living communally, supporting each other and attending to the daily chores together. At this time the community was almost self-sufficient: they grew wheat and processed it in their own mill; they grew all their vegetables and killed their own meat. The only food they brought in was poultry. Everyone hated chook day when they had to kill and pluck dozens of birds. However, nobody had to buy their own supplies (although, by the same token, you couldn't just go into the kitchen and help yourself if you got hungry).

By now the people wore uniforms. It was put to the women that the standardised blue dresses would be cheaper than mufti. The women agreed; it would mean they didn't have to buy their own fabric, and they had no money anyway – money was allocated according to the number of children each couple had, and was given to the husband to buy personal items the community couldn't provide, such as shoes and toiletries. The community itself was careful with money, and when they wanted to carry out a project such as putting up a new building, they would look at the shopping lists and work out what they could do without.

Neville was the sole leader, despite having twelve 'shepherds' who were supposed to have leadership roles as well, but in fact he brooked no opposition, nor was he often shown it. Sandy's mother Naomi was called in once as witness against a young man and when she came out she said to one of the men, 'That went wrong in there.'

He just said, 'Don't worry, sweetie. He's the boss and God's still on his throne.'

People had to be very careful if they didn't want to be called in to a men's meeting.

Phil managed to survive by keeping busy, by always having several projects on the go, and by striving with everything he had to make the money to keep the community afloat. He didn't stop to wonder how long he could keep going, he just put his head down and worked. But sooner or later something had to give.

CHAPTER FIVE: DESPERATION

All the people must obey the leaders in the Church in all things
and submit themselves willingly to them as unto the Lord ...
WHAT WE BELIEVE, P. 52

Neville held services twice a week, preaching his interpretation of the word of God. He was a powerful orator, striding up and down, using effective pauses, rhetorical questions, and expansive arm gestures to bring his message to his people. He was the only one who could show them the way to salvation, and how much God required of them. It was never easy to lead a selfless life, but their reward would come in heaven, whereas sinners would be denied a place at the right hand of God. He reinforced the moral precepts of the community: contraception was evil, divorce anathema, homosexuality and pre-marital sex forbidden. The world outside was a place of wickedness, wantonness, corruption, crime and selfishness.

At mealtimes Neville read aloud from the newspapers any items that confirmed his portrayal of the outside world, and so the people sitting at the long tables ate to the accompaniment of stories of murder, robbery and immorality. Nobody but Neville spoke at table.

The pressures on Phil mounted steadily as Neville demanded

more and more money. The business could no longer meet these increasing demands, which put Phil in an invidious position: his father wanted the money and it was Phil's duty as his son to provide it. Phil dealt with the problem by sending fictitious invoices to Clive Bilbie who, in good faith, paid the money into the community's account. Phil would then try to get the orders, in order to pay Clive back.

Phil was pulled between guilt at cheating his friend and fear of his father's wrath if he didn't provide the money Neville demanded. He worked every available minute, but the stress of the situation never eased. He knew that once a bogus invoice had been made good, his father would come demanding more money and the cycle would begin again.

Neville's rules governed every aspect of life, including how to bring up the children. He ordered that any child wetting the bed was to be put immediately into a cold shower, and the next day, instead of eating the evening meal, was to sit on the stage with his or her back to the entire community while they ate. Phil was horrified and stood up to his father about it in a men's meeting. Neville told him to sit down and shut up. 'Just because you're my son, it doesn't give you the right to question my authority.'

Phil didn't argue – there was no point – but he was determined that his kids wouldn't suffer such inhumane treatment and told Sandy they weren't going to obey the rule and they simply wouldn't tell Neville if any of the kids wet the bed. However, one night Phil came home late for dinner to find Israel sitting on the stage with his back to the dining room.

The prime reason for the rule, Phil believes, was to humiliate the parents, but the sense of shame for the children must have been enormous.

Sandy had felt compelled to tell Neville, and there was also the tell-tale sheet to explain, because Neville always asked the laundresses to tell him who had sent wet sheets to be washed. Phil started washing their sheets himself, and told Sandy that never again would one of their children be punished for wetting the bed. He knew that although she didn't say so, she was relieved.

Sandy's mother Naomi recognised the strength of her daughter's convictions but thought she was loyal to a fault.

But as time went by, Phil had even less to spend with his family as Neville's demands for money continued. Phil was manipulating the money, trying to appease Neville, and becoming increasingly guilt-ridden at lying to the friend who trusted him.

One day he went looking for his father to talk to him about a business matter and found him in bed with Gloria and a couple of the teenage girls. It made Phil sick to his stomach. Phil was fairly certain that Neville didn't go so far as to have intercourse with the girls, but he was certainly using them sexually. Phil also hated that his father was dishonouring Gloria, and knew that she must be in torment over what was happening.

However, it was a simple thing that made him take stock and question it all. He was driving back from Picton to the community and stopped at Kaikoura as he often did because he loved the sea. He'd just sit and look at it, or wander along the beach for a bit. He found himself watching a crab in a rock-pool and thinking that here he was, working all the hours he could, and he'd never be able to take his kids to the beach when he wanted to and let them find a crab. What was it all about? Who was he really working for? He had no answer, but it was another defining moment.

He got back home, unsettled and no closer to solving his problems. There was no respite from Neville who demanded yet more money: $100,000 for another building project.

Phil made up an invoice. Within 24 hours, Clive had put the money in the community's account and Phil just hoped he'd be able to make the order. Two or three days later, he broke. It was too much, trying to live with the pressure of the lies, having to make money and working so hard he never saw his family. All this in the name of Christianity, of God? He didn't know any more whether there even was a God.

Phil wanted out.

He didn't have a plan. He couldn't think beyond the fact that he needed to go. He decided to take Israel with him, both for the company and to show at least one of his children a bigger world than the one they lived in. He rang a friend who agreed to pick them up from the main road, and left a note under his office phone for Sandy and his father.

He drove one of the vans down to the next property and left it there in the gateway. For seven-year-old Israel it was all a huge adventure. He was going on a trip with his dad who was making it fun as they waited for their ride. 'Let's play a game, son. Every time we hear a car coming we'll hide in the grass.'

Israel loved it, but Phil was asking himself why a grown man would need to hide from his own father, and yet he knew. It was fear of being caught: fear of the men's meetings. He wasn't thinking that he was leaving for good. He just needed to get away from the pressure of living with the deceit he'd created.

The friend picked them up and drove them to Christchurch Airport. This foray into the outside world entranced Israel. The driver of the car wore a jacket made of leather. He smelt different from anyone Israel had encountered before. It was scary, but he was with his dad so he felt safe.

The friend gave them the tickets he'd booked and only a couple of hours after Phil had rung asking for help, they boarded a flight for Wellington.

Israel was deeply impressed that his dad knew all these people on the outside – that he knew where to go at the airport and what to do. The plane trip astonished him because he was given lollies and little packets of nuts. Wellington amazed him, too, with its tall buildings and all the people such as he'd never seen before.

They went to stay with Clive and Sue Bilbie. Phil confessed to Clive what he had done, and told him he wanted to sort the mess out. Clive understood the pressures Phil had been under and agreed to give him time to do it.

A few days after Phil's departure, Neville sent his daughter Charity to Wellington to reason with her brother. Phil let her take Israel back but he himself refused to return, despite her efforts to persuade him.

Phil was the eighth of Neville's 15 children to leave the community. Faith, Mercy, John, Michael, David, Daniel and Christian had all left earlier. John left his wife and children behind.

Phil veered between euphoria at being away from the community and fear that he'd never see his family again, but he couldn't go back to that small, caged world of work, conformity and meetings. To go back would be like a butterfly going back into its cocoon. For the first time in his life he felt free. It was November 1989. He was 27 years old and ready to fly.

CHAPTER SIX:
EXTREME MEASURES

*I forsake any family members ... who would in any way influence
me contrary to the commandments of Christ and his Apostles,
and contrary to the way of life of the Church at Springbank.*
WHAT WE BELIEVE, P. 24

Although Phil decided almost immediately that he wouldn't go back to Springbank, he wanted to clear up the financial mess he'd left behind him. He asked Neville to let him keep working for the community until the money was paid back. That way he might be able to keep in touch with his family, too. But, true to form, Neville refused to have anything to do with a son who broke the rules. 'We don't need you. You got us into this mess. We'll get ourselves out.'

Clive hadn't wanted to take the matter to court, but Neville's intransigence left him with no alternative.

Around this time Gloria became ill. She'd been suffering from headaches but now she became mute. Neville rang some of his eight children outside the community, blaming her illness on the shock of Phil's departure. Phil didn't believe he was the cause of his mother's illness but not being there to help and comfort her added to the pain of missing his family. One of his sisters still at

Springbank stood up to Neville and insisted on her mother seeing a doctor. She was diagnosed with an incurable brain tumour and hospitalised. Neville took her back to the community to be cared for.

Faith rang her father to ask his permission to visit her mother in hospital. His reply was typical: 'No, and why would she want to see *you*?'

The boys didn't ask; they just went. Gloria was very happy to see them, but she became agitated for fear that Neville would come and find them there. She lived for another 12 months, dying the following year in March 1991 at the age of 57. None of her children who had left the community were allowed to go to her funeral. Michael heard of her death only after she had been buried. He went on a rampage through Christchurch, smashing plate glass windows with his bare hands.

Now that Phil was out of the community, his own family was constantly on his mind. He rang them every night, but he had no idea what he was going to do about them. Neville applied pressure wherever he could. One night Sandy rang Phil to say that Crystal needed glasses but there was no money to buy them. For Phil, it was a very clear message from Neville: *It's your fault that there's no money and look what it's doing to your daughter.* Knowing what his father was doing didn't lessen the guilt he felt at his daughter being deprived of something she needed.

It was a cunning move on Neville's part because he knew Phil would tell Clive who might then be more lenient about the money. Clive, though, was keen to work out a solution. He arranged a meeting with Neville, offering him a deal whereby the community would supply him with $100,000 worth of stock over the next six months. Phil felt relieved; it was a generous offer because the community would only have to find about $30,000 for the materials. But again Neville rejected it. Clive had no choice but to take the matter to court.

Over the next 12 months, Phil watched the thriving company he'd built up dwindle and die. None of the people he'd built relationships with were prepared to deal with Neville who demanded that things always be done his way.

Shortly after the meeting between Clive and Neville, Phil's efforts to maintain a relationship with his children suffered a blow. One night when he rang, Sandy said, 'There's someone here who wants to talk to you.'

It was one of the leaders who said, 'It is in the best interests of everyone for you to have no contact with the children any more.'

Phil was utterly devastated, seeing it as another of his father's games of control, as if he was waiting for Phil's next move. What would his son do? Where would he take things from here? But it wasn't a game for Phil. These were his children and he would not allow his father to deny him access to them. He decided to get them out. But he couldn't simply walk in and pick up the kids. He knew that one way or other, Neville would prevent him. The only chance of success lay in abducting the five of them in a midnight raid. He wouldn't be able to take Sandy at the same time, but he reasoned he'd have a much stronger chance of her coming out later if he had the children.

In December 1989 Phil left the Bilbies' home where he'd been living since leaving the community, and went to Christchurch where he worked on the abduction plan for two weeks. He was careful, checking every last detail, knowing he'd only have this one chance. If he bungled it, he knew Neville would hide the children from him, deny that he knew where they were, and make sure Phil never got to see them again. Phil also knew his father would have the means and the power to do this successfully.

Phil enlisted the help of his friend Mark and his brothers John and David who had also left the community. Since he'd helped build the accommodation blocks, Phil had the advantage of knowing the layout by heart, and he planned to switch off the electricity mains to help with the getaway. He knew, too, how Neville's mind worked and he suspected his father would have moved the family to different rooms. He had an older friend inside the community, a strong-minded woman who still acted according to her own conscience, and he knew she would tell him where his family were. Through her, he learned that Neville had moved them to two small rooms, with Sandy and her mother Naomi sleeping in the inner room, and the children in the room that led off a courtyard.

It couldn't have been better for Phil. The driveway ran past the rooms and it would only be a matter of jumping a fence, stealing across the small courtyard, and entering the building. He didn't think the courtyard door would be locked because the community never locked its doors, but he couldn't be sure Neville wouldn't have changed that rule and he'd forgotten to ask his friend.

The four men drove two cars to the community at midnight. It was a risky venture and Phil kept hammering the point that this was their one chance: bungle it and he'd lose his kids forever. He was very focussed, very determined that this would work. The moon was nearly full and the night much brighter than he'd reckoned on but there was no turning back now.

It would be too noisy to drive the cars up the gravel driveway so, as planned, they left one parked on the roadside in the shadow of the pine trees on the far side of the road, and pushed the other one backwards up the drive, leaving it outside the children's room, ready for a quick getaway. Even so, the crunch of wheels on the gravel sounded horribly loud.

Mark, Dave and John waited beside the car while Phil slipped through the complex to turn off the electricity mains. Moonlight would help any pursuers once they got outside, but they'd lose time stumbling about in the darker buildings.

Phil ran back to where the others waited for him. A brief nod, and they were off. Mark waited in the car, ready to take off the moment they had the children. Phil and his brothers vaulted the fence and crept across the courtyard, over the chalk drawings the children had left there.

The courtyard door was shut. Phil's mind spun. What would he do if it was locked? But it opened. They were in. He stepped into the room, scanning it quickly. The kids were there, top and tailing in the two beds, a blond head at each end. He set about waking them. If they cried or shouted, he was sunk. He shook Israel's shoulder. 'Israel. Wake up. It's Dad come to get you.' Israel didn't say a word as his father picked him up, wrapping a blanket around him before passing him to Dave who ran with him out to the car. Now for the girls.

'Dawn, it's Dad come to get you.'

'It's okay, Justine. It's Dad.'

'Tendy, wake up, sweetie. Dad's come to get you.'

What astonishes him now is that not one of the children cried out or said a word. Israel and Justine only remember thinking, Oh, it's Dad. It's okay then. Israel remembers, too, the brightness of the moon as his uncle carried him out to the car.

But there were only four of them in the room. Phil had gambled on all five of them being together, but Crystal wasn't there, and if he didn't take her then, he would lose her forever. John and David settled the girls into the back of the car with Israel while Phil went through into the adjoining room where he knew Sandy would be. She and Naomi were asleep in the double bed with Crystal between them. He would have to wake Sandy. If she woke later to discover Crystal missing, and then the others … he couldn't do it. He put his hand on his wife's shoulder. 'Sandy – it's Phil.'

She woke, startled. 'What are you doing? What are you doing? You shouldn't be here!'

'I know. I just wanted to hold Crystal for a minute and give her a cuddle.'

But the disturbance woke Naomi who realised immediately what he intended to do. She yelled at Sandy not to hand over the baby – that he would take her. But Sandy, trained to be obedient to her husband, passed Crystal over. 'It's all right. He's her father.'

Phil took the baby and ran. Naomi leapt out of bed and grabbed hold of his arm, hauling him back. David tore through the door, shouldered her out of the way, and the two men raced out, jumped the low fence, piled into the car, and roared off down the drive. Behind them, they could hear people yelling and stumbling around in the dark. The whole operation had taken about two minutes.

They stopped at the second car to let Dave and John out, then all drove back to Christchurch to Faith's house. Israel remembers being in the back of the car with the other kids, and his father turning around from the front seat with a huge grin on his face. For Phil, the adrenalin was pumping.

It was later that the realisation of what he'd done and the enormity of it, hit him. He suffered huge guilt about taking the children from their mother the way he had. He had wanted to rescue them from Neville and the community, but to snatch

Crystal from her mother's arms was another matter entirely. He had betrayed the trust with which Sandy had handed Crystal to him. The only comfort was that he intended to get her out as well. She loved the children and she loved him, a belief reinforced by what she'd said to him that night, how she'd been concerned for him, and worried that he'd get into trouble if he was discovered.

The raid was a success, but Phil hadn't planned what to do next. He was 27 years old with five children aged from eight years to 16 months, and he had no idea how to care for them. He stayed with Faith and Alan for several weeks. They had nine children of their own but they took him in and worked hard to help him learn to be a good parent. Faith knew exactly what he was in for and tried to prepare him. It had been hard enough for her and Alan when they left with the five they had at the time, but at least they had been together, whereas Phil was on his own. For Faith the question to wrestle with had been what to believe; what was right. For Phil it was how to care for his children.

By now, Faith had worked through her own questions, facing each in turn and applying her formidable mind to finding the right answer for herself and her family. A generous person like Phil, she lived her religion by giving of herself. Her brother was in need so she took him and his family in, extending to him the benefit of her own hard-won experience. She would sit up all night with him, talking, trying to get him to understand what it meant to be responsible for five young children. She and their brother David wanted Phil to get a domestic purposes benefit so that he could stay home with the children, but he wanted to be up and doing.

It was as if he was driven. He'd escaped from his father physically; he was free to do what he wanted in the world – free to show Neville that he didn't need him – but for Phil that meant being out in the world, working and making things happen. He had so much energy, so many plans, and here was the chance to live his own life, and to give this wider life to his children. He would stay positive for them and show them that if they wanted something, they could get it. Sure, there were difficulties in the way, but all they had to do was work out ways of overcoming them.

The children loved their father uncritically and unconditionally: he was their leader and their hero.

Phil applied for a state house, and two months after they had moved in with Faith and Alan, one became available in Linwood in Christchurch. He moved his family from his sister's busy, organised house to one with no furniture and no one else to care for the children.

Now that they were on their own with just their father, the children began to experience the loneliness of life outside the community. For the first time in their lives they had only each other, and their father when he was at home. This new house was tiny, but it felt huge and empty. Here there was no aunt or big cousin to run to for comfort; there was nobody else to play with, and nothing in the house. It was bare, and so quiet. Israel tried not to show how much he was missing his mother. Dawn cried for her constantly, Tender-Joy was bewildered, and intrepid Justine was uncharacteristically quiet. Crystal was too young for anybody to really know how she felt, and she was too young to understand the promises Phil kept repeating: Don't worry, I'll get your mum back. We'll be a family again.

Phil began teaching them more about the outside world. He taught them the names for the days of the weeks and the months of the year. The older ones found it confusing to begin with and would ask him, 'Dad, what's second day called?'

He would tell them it was Monday and together they would recite the names of the days, then go on to name the months.

He gave them quizzes. 'Israel, what month is your birthday?'

'Sec – no, February!'

'Dawn, when's yours?'

'September. But it used to be ninth month.'

Much more quickly they learnt the denominations of money and what it would buy them. Much of the responsibility for his siblings fell on Israel's shoulders because the only way Phil could see to care for his children was to make money. Faith and David tried to convince him that he needed to be at home, but he had too much energy to stay confined there. The world was his and he knew he could make things happen, knew he could create the dream life for his children. Leading by example, he would show them that their opportunities were limitless. To do that, though, he had to go out into the world. He settled the older children into school and would take Tendy and Crystal with him in the car when he went out sourcing materials for waterbeds which he would make at home in the evenings. However, sometimes he would leave Israel in charge of the younger ones, occasionally leaving them alone at night.

Israel felt the responsibility keenly. For the first time in his life he discovered that food didn't automatically appear on the table three times a day, and besides, this house had no table. The five of them had been uplifted from a place of plenty where they were fed and cared for, to a small, dingy house where they were alone with nothing. They had no money; at eight years old Israel had to field callers such as the power company demanding payment. If the kids asked their dad for money to go to the shops, Phil had to tell them that there wasn't any. Israel could see that his father was busy, that he was trying with all he had to make enough money for them to live on.

Money! It fascinated Israel. Until that first trip to Wellington with his father, he'd never heard of it, and had no idea that you could take these special pieces of paper and metal into shops and exchange them for things you wanted. He pestered his father for answers. How did money work? How did you get it? Where did it come from? Who made it and why couldn't Dad just invent a machine that would produce money? Why did some people have a lot of money and they didn't? Where did the people with a lot of money keep it?

He experienced the dark side of not having enough of it, so partly understood why their father left them to go and find ways of earning it. The stress, the worry and responsibility gave Israel sharp stomach pains but he didn't tell his father who had enough problems. Instead, he looked forward to the time when he'd be able to stop worrying where the next meal for his sisters would come from. Money was the answer. His dad would make sure everything turned out right; he'd get them money and he'd get their mum back. Sometimes Israel dreamed of making enough money to buy the community so that their mother could be with them again. Money was the answer. It would make them all happy again.

CHAPTER SEVEN:
'I PROMISE WE'LL GET HER OUT.'

That night when Dad took us out of the community was the beginning of the journey of the next six years. From that moment on there was always the sense that we were escaping or fleeing something. ISRAEL

I remember all the moving around and there was always someone with us. Dad used to be constantly on the lookout, thinking someone from the community was going to come and get us, like at night time, the same as he did. TENDY (TENDER-JOY)

Phil was determined to make good his promise of getting Sandy out. He kept reassuring the kids and telling them not to worry, they'd be a proper family again. But he knew how strongly Sandy believed in Neville's preachings. He knew she believed that the only way to eternal salvation was to live in his community. Getting her out would be easy compared with the difficulty of keeping her out. He reasoned that if he could break Neville's hold over her, then she would be only too happy to stay with her children and with him. He knew, too, that Sandy wouldn't listen to his arguments. He needed to find somebody who knew how to deprogramme people who had come out of cults. The nearest person his research turned up was a woman in Australia, and thanks to a friend who paid her expenses, he arranged for her to come to New Zealand in early February to work with Sandy. Phil planned to abduct his wife to coincide with the day the woman arrived in Christchurch.

As a precaution, Phil took the children up to Auckland to stay with friends who had left the community. The distance from Christchurch had several advantages: if Sandy ran away from him, she wouldn't be able to take the children back to the community with her, but the greatest advantage was that the woman would be able to talk to Sandy while they travelled north in the car. Sandy would have no choice but to listen. With the help of his brother Michael, Phil worked out a plan to abduct Sandy at night. They kept it simple: they would just walk in and escort her out, carrying her if necessary. By now the community had a night watchman so the two men had to be more careful than when Phil had taken the children.

They crept into the accommodation block, slipped into Sandy's room, and shone the torch on the bed, only to find a different woman asleep in it. They flicked off the torch and backed out, praying that she wouldn't wake. It would all be over if she gave the alarm. She stirred but didn't wake as they eased the door shut. What to do now? Sandy could be in any of the dozens of rooms in the two buildings that made up the complex. They had to get her that night. The woman from Australia was waiting at Faith's house but, more than that, Phil didn't think he could bear the disappointment of failing to rescue her.

He led the way out of the building and they hid behind a wall till the watchman went past. Phil's mind was in overdrive, but in the end he knew his only hope of success was to ask his friend inside the community where Sandy was. He went to her room, hoping her quarters hadn't been changed as well. But she was there and happy to tell him. Neville had taken precautions against another raid by moving Sandy to a different building.

The two men sneaked inside, finding the right room with no further problem. For the second time in as many months, Phil woke his wife in the dead of night. He was expecting her to shout at him, demanding to know where her children were.

'Sandy,' he whispered, one eye on Naomi still asleep beside his wife, 'I've come to get you.'

She didn't speak – just got straight up, but the disturbance woke Naomi who ordered her daughter to have nothing to do with Phil and to get back into bed.

Phil tensed, ready to grab his wife and run, but Sandy told her mother to be quiet and she walked out of the room with her husband and brother-in-law, still wearing her pyjamas.

The three of them tiptoed through the complex with Phil not quite believing it had been so easy. He'd been sure she would be angry with him, but she got into the car as if this were an ordinary trip. She wanted to know about the children: were they all right and where were they?

He reassured her that they were doing fine, and yes, he would take her to the friends they were staying with in Auckland and in the meantime they needed to go to Faith's house to pick up the clothes he'd organised for her. He didn't tell her about the de-programmer who was also waiting at Faith's.

It was well after midnight by the time they'd picked up the clothes and the woman, but Phil wanted to get out of Christchurch, away from Neville's vicinity. Taking Michael with them for added security, he drove to a motel in a small town a couple of hours north, with the woman talking to Sandy the entire time. They were exhausted when they arrived. Michael slept what was left of the night across the doorway outside Sandy's room.

In the morning, Phil knocked on her door but there was no answer. He flung the door open to find that she was gone. She would have had to climb over Michael to creep from the motel. He didn't know if she'd even been to sleep. How long had she been gone? Had she had time to ring the community to ask somebody to come and get her? They leapt in the car, tore all over the town searching for Sandy, and found her eventually in a phone booth. By repeating that he was taking her to the children, Phil persuaded her to get back in the car. The children exerted a stronger pull at that moment than returning to the community.

They continued the drive north to Picton with the woman trying to reason with Sandy; her children needed their mother; she wanted to be their mother and she couldn't be if she stayed in Neville's church. The woman's arguments were eloquent and persuasive, but Sandy's loyalty to Neville and her belief that she could only serve God in his church were equally strong. Phil drove, listened, and swung between hope and despair.

They took the ferry to Wellington and stayed that night with the Bilbies whose lifestyle must have seemed to Sandy the epitome of worldliness and so helped to confirm for her that she was right to shun the world. Clive, a kindly, benign father-figure, so different from Neville, tried to reason with her, too, but she kept saying, 'I've got to serve God. I've got to do what's right.'

Phil despaired. Sandy was torn between what she wanted to do and what she felt she must do. He could only hope that her love for her children would prove stronger than her belief that the only way she could serve God was to return to Neville.

They left for Auckland the next day, a long drive for a woman who hadn't been far outside the community since she was 16. Phil couldn't work out whether or not the deprogrammer was making any impression on Sandy. One moment he thought she was winning but the next moment it seemed that Sandy was rejecting everything she said. As arranged, he dropped the woman off at Auckland Airport.

Always the optimist, Phil talked to Sandy about how much the kids were looking forward to seeing her. Surely when she saw them she would be able to leave Neville behind.

His spirits lifted as he watched her reunion with her children. It was all he had hoped it would be, proving to him how much she loved and wanted to be with them. Tendy, particularly, clung to her and wouldn't let her out of her sight. Israel, Dawn and Justine had so much to tell her. Phil watched his family and knew he'd done the right thing in reuniting them. Sandy hugged them and told them how they'd grown, they'd changed – and she was so pleased to see them. She held Crystal close as if she was afraid her baby would vanish if she set her down.

Sandy's attitude towards Phil gave him hope, too. Instead of the reproaches he still half-expected, she was making every effort to be friendly towards him. Later he realised she had believed that they would all return to the community with her.

But the set-up of five small children in a caravan, along with a husband who had to participate in the outside world, was an impossible situation for Sandy. The combination of her extreme loyalty, naïvety and deep religious conviction, made her feel besieged in the outside world where people bombarded her with ideas and information so contrary to Neville's teachings. It didn't help when business contacts kept calling Phil, assuming he was still heading the community waterbed business. He had to keep explaining that he now had nothing to do with it. Sandy saw such contacts as influencing him to turn away from the God she believed in. She believed utterly in Neville's teachings of an evil outside world. Salvation, he taught, was only possible if she lived in his community. Cunningly, his teachings also decreed that children would be saved even if only one of their parents led a true and Godly life with him in the community.

Once Sandy understood that Phil wasn't going back and wouldn't let the children return either, she believed that their only hope of salvation was for her to sacrifice herself by giving them up and going back without them. The tug between wanting to be with her children and feeling she had to serve God made her increasingly unhappy. Phil's own situation was precarious: he could offer her life in the caravan in Auckland or in the bare house in Christchurch. He reluctantly accepted that the only thing to do was to let her return to Neville's community. He told her to ring them. They paid for her air ticket and she flew back without her children.

As always, Phil refused to accept defeat. The children were upset but not devastated, having complete faith in their father when he said, 'Don't worry, kids. We'll get Mum back. We'll all be a family again.' He drove them back to Christchurch, staying cheerful and optimistic so that the children remembered the joy of seeing their mother, rather than grieving because she had chosen to leave them. Their dad was their hero, the one who would never abandon them, the one who would make things right. He gave them hope. He promised he'd get their mum back and they knew he would do it. On the long drive south he kept them occupied by singing to them, stopping at parks to let them play, and playing games with number plates as they drove.

All the time, Phil's mind was busy. Sandy had gone back because he hadn't thought things through and so he made a plan for what to do once he'd rescued her a second time. He was determined to learn from that first mistake. Back home in Christchurch, he threw his energy into devising a plan designed to let her live away from Neville and the community. He was determined to get her out again, but this time he would make it work.

He settled the older children into school then worked on the plan. He figured that if they had somewhere remote to live then Sandy wouldn't be worried about outside influences. There was still no money, either to put towards a plan to get her out, or to support and care adequately for the children who were finding life even harder now that they'd had the few days with their mother. Living conditions in the dingy little house were spartan because it was still completely devoid of furniture.

Phil typically saw the barrenness as a problem to solve. He had no spare money to buy anything, even from second-hand shops, so he scavenged for timber at the city dump. First he made water-beds for the children. Israel and Crystal slept in one room, Dawn, Justine and Tendy in the second bedroom, while he had the third. Gradually he scavenged more wood plus the odd, battered piece of furniture from the dump, but until he could make a table and find chairs and chests of drawers, the family sat on the floor and kept their clothes in suitcases. The children wore clothes given to them by their aunts, Faith and Mercy, as well as an odd collection from charity shops. They look back now and laugh at photographs of themselves dressed in hideous combinations of colour and style. The community which they'd come from wasn't strong on fashion and they had no idea of how to put a look together.

Even with the furniture Phil had made or scavenged, the house was always bare. The cupboards were, too. At first the children lived on bread and sometimes, for a treat, they'd have milk. As their father earned more money they ate things he could prepare easily, such as canned tuna, baked beans, and instant noodles. The one thing always in the cupboard was flour because it was cheap, but Phil was too busy to do anything with it. He didn't know how to cook and the children got used to the smell of burning whenever he did venture beyond the tins and instant noodles.

Israel had often been with his mother in the kitchen in the community, helping her rub butter into flour, mixing dough, and watching as she put batches of baking into the oven. From this grounding, he taught himself to cook, making pancakes and scones for his sisters, then trying more complicated recipes. All the children relished the variation in their diet, although there were a few disasters. Tendy created the most dramatic one. She wasn't quite four years old, but Israel's cooking impressed her. Early one morning she slipped out of bed and headed for the kitchen to make breakfast. It looked easy and she knew that cooking involved getting things out of the cupboards. She took out all the cooking utensils, found a bowl almost as big as she was, and set about copying what she'd seen Israel doing – putting things into the bowl and mixing them up with the big spoon. In went the flour, the dried macaroni, instant noodles, vegemite, bread and milk. She was busy stirring when the family discovered her. She looked up at them, her blond hair tousled and her smile wide. 'I'm cooking.'

Phil cleaned up the mess. Even his younger children had picked up the 'you can do anything' attitude he was intent on instilling in them; all the same, he hoped Tendy wouldn't try cooking by herself again until she had a few more skills.

The sense of responsibility weighed on Israel. It seemed it was up to him to make sure his sisters had food in this strange new world where meals didn't automatically appear three times a day. He worried that there would be nothing for them to eat the next day, or even at the next meal. He accepted that his stomach pains were part of this new life.

Phil, knowing that the best thing he could do for his children was to give them back their mother, threw all his energy into making sure this second attempt to get her out would succeed. She'd been so upset by the worldly influences that he felt it would be best if they could live away from the outside world.

Accordingly, he put an ad in the paper seeking to rent a bach in an isolated part of the upper Marlborough Sounds. A Christian couple, Wes and Ellen, replied, and when they heard his story told him he could have the bach rent-free. They were his miracle.

There were many more obstacles to overcome, but Phil was extremely focussed; he would solve the difficulties one at a time. He made lists, ticking off each item as he achieved it.

Wes and Ellen took him and the children up to the Sounds to see the bach. It was ideal because the only access was by water which meant nobody could creep up on them. The drawback was that Phil now needed a boat, and he'd had no boating experience. He needed money to buy a boat and he had none. He added the boat, the boating know-how, and the money to his list. He took a course and got his marine certificate, ticked that off. Did a first-aid course and ticked that off, too. Making the money to buy a boat was the easiest of all. He knew how to make waterbeds so that was what he did. He set up a workshop in the lounge, and in the evenings he made the beds, getting the children to help with the assembly. The children loved helping; they thrived on having him around and doing things with him. It was exciting, too, because they knew that all this effort was to get their mother back.

The suppliers Phil had dealt with when he was in the community knew his story and helped him by giving him the mattresses for nothing. He would finish a bed, put an ad in the paper, and sell it the following day. By the end of March he had $20,000.

Meanwhile, he wanted his kids to keep in contact with their mother and would drop them off for weekend visits at the community. In effect, Phil was saying to his father, *You can't stop them seeing their mother and if you try holding on to them you know what I'll do.* What he would have done was go straight to the media and blast the whole story across every front page in the country. Both men by now were well aware of the power of the media and Phil knew his father clearly understood the amount of negative attention that would be generated if the community were to be involved in such publicity.

Eight-year-old Israel was terrified during those visits to the community. It was wonderful seeing their mum again, and all of the children looked forward to being with her each weekend, but he was old enough to be aware of the tense undertones of the visits. He knew from Neville's preaching that outsiders were evil, wicked people, and now he and his sisters were the outsiders. All the time they were in the community, he felt people were looking at them, thinking how bad they were. He knew that this was the place they'd had to escape from, so the people here must be evil, even though he'd never heard his dad say so, and their mum had come back there to live, so how could they be? It was very confusing for a young boy with such a keen sense of responsibility.

Neville put a stop to the visits, telling Phil that it was too hard on the kids. Phil knew it wasn't about the kids; this was just another chapter in the battle between him and his father. His determination equalled his father's. His children were going to see their mother whether their grandfather liked it or not.

The following weekend he dropped them off out the front of the community, telling Israel, 'Go in and tell Mum you've come to see her.' Then he drove away.

Neville came out to meet them, bringing Sandy with him. He took one look at his five grandchildren standing hand-in-hand in front of him and launched into a tirade. Their father was evil. He was wicked. He had wrecked his children's lives by forcing them to live outside in the full wickedness of an evil world with him, their Godless father.

Israel was terrified. Dawn just wanted be with her mother and she tried to shut out her grandfather's shouting by clinging to her. Justine, Tendy and Crystal were too scared and too young to make sense of the outburst. They cried as Sandy held them while Neville repeated over and over: 'Your father is evil. He's wicked. Isn't he, Sandy?'

It was clear Sandy was torn between being Neville's obedient, humble servant, and protecting her children. The only way she could do so was to hold them and nod in response to Neville's ranting. She was careful not to verbally support what he was saying, and when she was alone with her children she never repeated any of his accusations against Phil. But the entire weekend was tainted. None of them could relax, even when Neville wasn't around, and they were frightened to let Sandy out of their sight.

When Phil picked them up two days later they were a mess. He loaded them into the car, but before he could get in, Neville came out with the men and surrounded him. With the children cowering in the car, Neville gave the order, 'Gather round, men. Let's cast the demons out of this guy.'

Above the melee of shouts and shaking fists, Phil heard one of the men yell, 'Why don't you get down on your knees and beg forgiveness?'

'If that's what it takes,' Phil said, 'then I'll do it.'

They laughed.

He drove away, knowing that in the eyes of the community he was unforgiven and unforgivable.

All the way back to Christchurch he worked at reassuring the children: 'Everything's going to be okay, kids. Don't worry, you don't have to go back there again. Don't worry, we'll get your mum out. We'll get her out.'

Neville's diatribe didn't change the way the children felt about their father. Israel remembers his calming presence in the car on the way home. They could relax. They were with their conquering hero, their rescuer, their dad.

Phil never took them to the community again, but he was more determined than ever that Neville wasn't going to win. He would get Sandy out and the children would have their mother again.

He bought a boat for $15,000. Next he enrolled the children in the Correspondence School, had suitably modest clothes made for Sandy, and set the bach up. Everything was ready, except that he still hadn't devised a plan to get her out and he considered another midnight raid too risky.

He devised and discarded plan after plan. Some he tried didn't work. He asked the doctor for sedatives strong enough to send a person to sleep. There was a video night coming up in the community which would leave the accommodation blocks empty for the evening. The plan was for his younger brother David to sneak in, put a bottle of spiked water beside Sandy's bed, and hide until she fell asleep. He would then call Phil on the mobile and together they would carry her out. David got into her room without any problem but heard somebody coming before he had a chance to put the water beside the bed. He scarpered, managing to get out without being caught.

Another time Phil heard that Sandy had a dentist's appointment. He arranged for an accomplice to go to the waiting room and let him know when she arrived. Neville got wind of it and Sandy didn't keep the appointment.

In the end Phil decided to kidnap Sandy when she was away from the community during the day, going to a fake doctor's appointment he would set up for her, ostensibly a consultation about her ongoing eye problems.

The community doctor was the friend Phil had built the kitchen for years before, and although he knew very well that helping Phil meant he'd lose thousands of dollars in business – because Neville would cut off anyone who helped his son – he didn't hesitate, and set up the appointment immediately.

With the day and time sorted, Phil went back to the planning. It was exciting to devise an intricate plot, and that it was against his father lent extra spice. He hired a plain white car and a police uniform, asked a friend's 21-year-old son to play the part of the policeman, and even wrote him a script of what to say when he pulled Sandy's car over. Phil didn't tell Faith or any of his siblings except Michael what he intended to do, for fear they would try and talk him out of it.

The planning had taken weeks but by April 1990 it was all complete. Phil didn't begrudge the effort or time he put in, as it showed his children to what lengths he would go to get their mother back, and would also show his wife that he loved her and wanted her. He believed utterly that he was right to abduct Sandy; the issue wasn't so much about taking her away from where she wanted to be, as giving her back to her children. She would be happy in the supportive environment he'd gone to so much trouble to create. Their children would be happy with Sandy free to be the loving mother he knew she wanted to be. All they needed was time away from the influence of the community, time for him to show Sandy that life on the outside didn't have to be the hell Neville's diatribes painted it. Phil didn't consider the legalities of what he was doing, probably because he'd grown up in a community where his father's word was above the law of the land. Out in the world it certainly wasn't illegal for a grown man to disobey his father. He saw that the end justified the means.

On the day before Sandy's appointment, Phil drove the children up to the bach at Blackwood Bay. He was so confident of the abduction succeeding that he told the children that Mummy was coming the next day. All of them were too excited to sleep much that night. By the morning Phil's confidence of the previous night had vanished. Would it work? Would the timing be right?

In fact the plan worked perfectly. Back in Canterbury, the 'policeman' intercepted the car in which Sandy and her minder were travelling. He stuck word for word to the script Phil had written: 'Are you Sandra Cooper, and are these the names of your children?' When she said, 'Yes', he told her she was wanted for questioning.

She got out of the community car and into the hired car, without asking for police ID. They made an incongruous couple, the fake police officer and the woman in her long, blue dress, headscarf and sensible shoes – she accepting the turn of events without suspicion. Phil had banked on the fact that she was used to obeying authority figures, but more than that, he knew that once she did begin to understand the situation, she would go along with it because she'd be concerned about her children. They drove off, the 'policeman' telling her that he was going to take her to them. He then made an official-sounding radio call to Phil to say they were on their way.

Phil still couldn't relax. It was a five-hour drive to Picton, and the 'policeman' had to stop to pick up Michael who again was acting as security, and the break might give Sandy the chance to escape. He knew, too, that seeing Michael would instantly give the game away because she knew him. Phil believes she must have suspected the truth but went along with the story because she wanted to see her children. She didn't speak or ask questions during the entire journey.

Phil waited til the car was about an hour away before he loaded the children into their 17-foot runabout. The trip to Waikawa Bay from the bach at Blackwood Bay took about 20 minutes, with the children straining their eyes all the way in case Mummy was already there and waiting for them. When they got to the jetty there was still some time to wait. Phil strove to be calm and reassuring although his nerves were stretched tight. What would he say to Sandy? How would he justify what he'd done?

Her car got to the marina at Waikawa Bay at about three in the afternoon. The 'policeman' kept to the script as Phil approached: 'Are you Philip Cooper?'

Phil wanted Sandy to feel that the whole exercise was official and under control because she had been so used to control in the community. But none of that mattered the minute she saw the children who raced towards her, smothering her with hugs, kisses, tears and questions.

All the way to the bach in the boat she cuddled and held them. She hadn't seen them for about two months.

The only thing that didn't go right was that the 'police officer' rolled the car on the way home. He wasn't hurt, but his mother found out what Phil had done and she was none too pleased.

CHAPTER EIGHT:
A TASTE OF PARADISE

No husband ever has the right to ask his wife or children to leave the Church and no Christian should ever leave the Church because he or she is asked to do so by any relative or family member. WHAT WE BELIEVE, P. 62

Sandy didn't speak to Phil during the boat trip. As he had expected, all her attention and love was for her children, but she was also treating him with reserve, seeming to distance herself from him. He would have some explaining to do later. He hoped she would be able to accept his reasons for kidnapping her.

The children had so much to tell their mother. Almost before his father had the chance to tie up the boat, Israel leapt onto the jetty, holding his hand out to help his mum climb up. He wanted to drag her off right that second to show her the bach and all the wonderful things inside it. There was so much he wanted her to see: the trees, the hills and the beach where they could swim. She had to see their dog too, a yappy little terrier called Rufus. Sandy laughed and hugged Israel. 'Wait,' she told him. 'It won't disappear. We can't leave the girls in the boat.'

Dawn picked Crystal up and passed her to her mother. Justine and Tendy scrambled out by themselves, and with Sandy carrying

Crystal, the four older children danced around her, all talking at once, wanting her to share their good fortune at having such a magical place to stay. But the best magic of all was having their mother with them again.

Sandy put the children to bed that night, making it clear to Phil that she didn't want any input from him. She prayed with them, read to them, and tucked them up. Dawn threw her arms around her mother's neck and clung to her. She'd missed her so much. Would she stay with them this time? She wanted to have her mum all the time. She wanted her to kiss her goodnight every night.

Sandy stroked her daughter's shoulder-length hair – how shockingly short it was – and told her how much she loved her. But she made no promises about staying. The children all slept in one room with four bunks, with Dawn and Crystal top and tailing. The four older children looked so like their father with their blond hair and Cooper features, whereas Crystal was a replica of Sandy herself, with darker hair and rounder face.

Sandy waited until they were all asleep before she spoke to Phil. Why had he taken her away from the community? He knew his explanation would be crucial if they were to have any chance of living together as a family. He kept it simple, not mentioning his father's name at all. The children missed her, he missed her, and he wanted them to be a family again. He hoped they'd be able to achieve that here where they would be free from outside influences. She seemed to accept his explanation, but whether she really did, or said she did because she was so happy to be with her children, he didn't know.

He didn't know, either, whether all his careful planning would succeed, but as he watched Sandy with her children he was hopeful; she loved them, there was no doubt about that. Everything was set up for success; she was secure in the little world he'd provided; she didn't have to deal with the outside and there were no pressures on her. All she had to do was be a mother. It only took a couple of days before she'd lost all her reserve with him and so began the happiest time of their married life.

Phil was still very careful not to put in her way any temptation to escape. He unplugged the phone and hid it. He didn't take the family near a town for several weeks. He and Sandy spent their days supervising the children's schoolwork, taking them for walks, and going fishing. There was no pressure and all he had to do was make sure he got enough food for them to survive, which he did by fishing and working the occasional day or two at the local salmon farm. When Sandy got frightened by the noise the possums made at night, Phil got out the shotgun and he and Israel went possum hunting. They relished their role as saviours and protectors of their women.

The bach was a paradise for the children. They were with their mother, their father was around most of the time, and the house was furnished with proper chairs, tables and couches. There were pictures on the walls and rugs on the floor. They hadn't experienced such comfort and luxury since leaving Faith's home months before.

Phil's relationship with Sandy was better than it had ever been. Neville wasn't there, hovering over them as a real or threatened presence, and they could both relax. They made love often, revelling in the freedom from all pressure. However, their community indoctrination meant they never discussed birth control because it was evil, in the same way that abortion and murder were evil. They didn't think about pregnancy, either. They were just two married people making love and would be happy with the consequences whatever they turned out to be.

Eventually they had to go into Picton for supplies. Phil was frightened that Sandy would run, so he took Israel aside and told him to make sure he always stayed with his mother. He knew it was putting a lot of responsibility on him, but he was counting on Sandy not taking just one child if she went back. She would go alone or not at all.

That first trip into town was an adventure for the children. They had never gone to town with their mother before – and they were going by boat! With one part of his mind, Phil listened to their chatter and to Sandy responding to them but, for him, the outing was an ordeal. He didn't want Sandy to feel he was watching her every move, but he knew it was risky to go where she might find a phone and ring the community. He understood very well the total control his father had over his followers and he knew that Sandy was still torn. On that trip, he made sure the seven of them stayed together, involving the children and Sandy in every purchase he made. On subsequent trips he was able to relax his vigilance as she seemed to be letting go of the community.

They went everywhere by boat, one day getting caught by the weather on the way back from fishing. The sea came up too rough for him to dock the boat and he had to take it round to the next bay where it was sheltered enough for Sandy and the children to jump into the water and wade ashore. From there they had to walk back through the trees to the bach. Life for the children was exciting, it was fun and they felt secure and happy, although Israel still suffered from the stomach pains that had started in Christchurch. Again he didn't mention them to his parents; they had enough to worry about. Even though life was idyllic on the surface, he knew there wasn't much money, and that lack of money meant lack of food. He watched his mother. She seemed happy and he hoped she'd be with them forever, but there was still that undercurrent of worry.

Friends and family came to visit. Wes and Ellen the bach-owners came, and Faith came up a couple of times with some of her family. They had never seen Sandy so relaxed and happy. This laughing woman was so different from the controlled Sandy of the community. Here she was at ease. She didn't even seem to worry about not going to church. To her there was only one true church and she couldn't attend it but she seemed content to read her Bible and pray each night with the children. Phil went along with her observances and didn't upset her by telling her that he now questioned the whole idea of God. It may be coincidence, but the photos and footage taken of the family's months at the bach all show Sandy without her headscarf, the community symbol of women's subservience to men.

The idyll couldn't last. Phil knew they would have to leave sooner or later, that they couldn't live in isolation forever. Part of him wanted more out of life anyway; he needed to be making things happen. After about three months they decided the time had come to re-enter the world. They discussed where they would live: would they settle in nearby Blenheim, or would they go back to Christchurch?

They talked it over with the children and together decided on Christchurch. They had the house to go back to, and such gear as they possessed, but more importantly they had family in Christchurch. It was a wrench to leave the bach where they'd been so happy but, as always, Phil was looking to the future and looking forward to making his way in the world. At the beginning of July 1990, he packed his family, the terrier, and all their luggage into the van and they set off for Christchurch.

Sandy grew quiet as soon as they began passing through populated areas. She turned away from worldly roadside hoardings advertising cafes, breweries and motels. Sights such as women wearing make-up and short skirts, which hadn't worried her on their trips to Picton, now seemed to distress her. Phil tried to engage her in talk about what they would do once they got home. She merely nodded in response and he suspected she didn't take in anything he said. The children sang the newest songs their mother had taught them and the dog leapt around. Phil was relieved when eventually the dog went quiet. Suddenly the kids started shrieking, 'Rufus has been sick! Rufus has been sick!' The smell was foul.

Tendy remembers the dog being sick and her father stopping on the side of the road, muttering something like, 'Oh, I can't …' then grabbing the shotgun and the dog and disappearing into the bush at the side of the road. The kids heard a shot and a yelp, then their father came back without the dog, got in and drove off as if nothing had happened, and they were all thinking, *Oh my gosh! Where's the dog?*

A vomiting dog was just too much for Phil to cope with, especially as Sandy grew quieter and more withdrawn the further south they travelled.

The move unsettled her badly. There were so many outside influences in Christchurch, so many decisions to make that she'd never had to think about before: what schools the children would go to, what supermarket she should shop at, what she would she cook for dinner – and what would she do about church?

The children helped her as much as they could, proud to show off their worldly knowledge, but Israel saw that she wasn't happy.

He kept his worries to himself. The others soon picked up their mother's mood. Dawn and Tendy clung to her skirts, unwilling to let her out of their sight, while Justine distressed her further by shows of disobedience which Sandy saw as rebellion and contrary to how a Christian daughter should behave. Crystal continued to be her normal happy self, sitting on the bare floor surrounded by the few toys and books the family had, and singing to herself.

Phil hoped for the best and dived back into work. He felt invigorated to be out in the world again, renewing business contacts and gathering materials to resume making waterbeds, but it was torture for Sandy. She reverted to wearing the blue community dress and headscarf she'd worn the day she was abducted. She hadn't worn the dress once in the Sounds.

Not long after they moved, Phil had to go to Wellington to discuss the court case concerning the $100,000 the community owed Clive. He had a morning appointment in Christchurch to install a waterbed. He reassured Sandy that he'd be back to say goodbye to her and pick up his bag in time for his afternoon flight. He was only going to be gone overnight. She rang him mid-morning and asked him to please come home at 12. Most unusually, she was insistent and he did as she asked.

He got home, but she wasn't in the kitchen or the living room. He searched the house and found her waiting for him in bed. She asked him to make love to her and later it seemed to him as if she'd been saying, *I love you. Please forgive me for what I'm going to do.* It was a significant event, since she'd never done anything like it before. Both of them had grown up with very Victorian attitudes about modesty and sex that hadn't changed in spite of Neville's actions. But at the time, Phil simply thought that it was his lucky day.

She'd packed his bag so that it was ready for him to take. She was the ideal wife.

Phil flew to Wellington and called home that evening but nobody answered. It was the same in the morning. He flew back to Christchurch late in the afternoon, sick to his stomach, and found the house in darkness. He had no key and had to break a window to get inside. Sandy had left a note on the table.

I'm sorry for what I've done. I've taken the kids but they're okay.

Phil was distraught but he understood her terrible dilemma: she wanted to be with him and the children, but living outside the community meant that she was rebelling against God and thus eternal salvation would be denied her. That, along with the pressures of everyday living had been too much. His guess is that she phoned the community as soon as he left.

He called his brother, John, telling him what had happened, and asked him to come over. Next, he phoned the community and asked to speak to Sandy. He was prepared for a refusal but she was allowed to come to the phone. He told her he was coming to pick the kids up. It was a short conversation.

By the time Phil and John got out to the community, it was late at night but the lights were on in the big dining room. They walked in to find Neville waiting for them, surrounded by all the men and half the rest of the community. Crystal was sitting on Sandy's knee with the other four children on either side of their mother. Phil felt the power of the set-up, but refused to be intimidated although the message was clear: *Philip, are you going to take these children from their mother – in front of witnesses?*

Phil ignored his father. He held the door open and said, 'Come on, kids, let's go.' All of them ran to him; even Crystal jumped off her mother's lap to go straight to her father.

Neville strode up with three or four men. 'Did that make you feel good?'

Phil said, 'I've got nothing to say to you.' He looked at Sandy and her face was torn.

She had to watch her children leave when all she needed was one word from Neville and she could have gone with them. Phil believed that Neville could have told her she'd be able to find eternal salvation anywhere as long as she lived a Christian life, but she was too valuable a tool in the ongoing battle with his son.

Phil drove away knowing yet again that he was a monster in the eyes of his wife and the community. The children were a mess of tears and questions: What's happening? Where's Mum?

It was the most heart-wrenching night of his life. He put his sobbing children to bed, all the time telling them not to worry, that he would get their mum back. Everything was going to be fine.

The kids cried themselves to sleep, and so did he. They had lost their mother again, and his attempts to create a family life for his children had failed.

He was a wreck. After the months of planning to get her out, he was back at square one and back to being a single dad. All that effort and time wasted. Those were tough nights for the children, too. They'd spent three wonderful months with their mother, only to have their security and happiness destroyed.

Faced with his distraught children and Sandy's intransigence, Phil thought seriously about giving in: packing them up and going back to the community. Part of him wanted to do just that, especially when he had to listen to the kids crying themselves to sleep. He worried most about seven-year-old Dawn and three-year-old Tendy. His oldest daughter was utterly heartbroken and took no comfort from his repeated assurances that he'd get her mum back again, while Tendy drifted about looking lost and wounded. Of the four girls, twenty-month-old Crystal appeared least affected and was quickly back to her happy, chirpy self. Justine who had not long turned five, and Tendy at not quite four, were old enough to feel the loss more acutely. Israel soon appeared to get over his mother's departure. Phil was proud of his capable son who was doing all he could to look after his sisters.

Israel continued to keep quiet about the stomach pains, which had worsened after his mother left. Why worry his dad when there was no money to go to a doctor anyway?

Although it was a struggle, Phil forced himself to keep hope in their lives. He told them over and over not to worry, that one day they would all be together again. For some time he wrestled with the question of whether he should sacrifice himself and just go back to the community with the kids. It would be torture for him, but it mightn't be so bad if the children had their mother again.

In the end, though, he knew he couldn't go back. He didn't want it for his children either. He had to keep moving forwards.

And so the planning started all over again.

CHAPTER NINE:
MYSTICAL PLACE AMONG THE STARS

When Dad told us we were going to America to live with the Hutterites I was so excited because I had memories of these men coming to the community dressed in their strange clothes and speaking with strange accents. They were held in such high esteem. I likened them to the three wise men in the Bible and I thought they lived in this mystical place among the stars. And when we got there it turned out to be pretty much like that. ISRAEL

The battle between Phil and his father took a new twist with Sandy's return to the community. Sandy discovered she was pregnant, but when she told Neville, he decreed that her baby would be born a bastard. The logic went something as follows: Sandy couldn't possibly be pregnant to a man who was as despicable as Phil, therefore she must have consorted with another man. Sandy was devastated but she bore the slur on her character as just punishment for staying so long out of the community.

Phil heard of her pregnancy and of his father's decree via the bush telegraph operating between the community and outside. If he'd needed any convincing that it would be worth another attempt to rescue his wife, this was it. His child would not grow up under the burden of such a stigma in a community where legitimacy mattered. His father would not win. The problem, though, was formidable. He was forced to recognise the strength of Sandy's enthralment to Neville and his teachings. She couldn't live independently and he had no idea how they might live, even if he was able to get her out for a third time.

He continued to reassure the children. 'Mum will come back. We'll get her back, don't worry.'

The crux of the problem, he decided, was that Sandy believed with all of her being that the only way she could achieve eternal salvation for herself and her children was to stay with Neville inside his community. Casting around for anything that might help, Phil remembered the Hutterite elders and how much his father had admired them. Although they'd severed their connection with Neville because of their disquiet at how he ran his community, Phil thought they might be able to persuade his father to let Sandy go. They were Godly men whom Neville respected, so perhaps he might listen to them. It was worth a try and he had no other ideas.

He wrote to the elders who had visited Neville's community, explaining who he was and what the problem was. They rang him, inviting him and Israel to come over to visit, and they paid for the tickets.

While Faith cared for the girls, Phil and Israel flew to America. While his dad talked to the elders, Israel was free to explore the community. It felt like home – like home had been back in the New Zealand community when Mum and Dad were both there. The women in their long dresses smiled at him and spoiled him with treats from their kitchens; the other kids played with him on the swings and slides, or took him on expeditions to streams and lakes. There were so many people. He felt he'd come home.

Phil discussed every aspect of the problem with the elders. After careful thought, they decided to send Neville a letter asking him to allow Sandy to be a mother to her children, basing their appeal on common decency. They had good reason to expect a favourable reply because of Neville's admiration for their way of life.

Neville's reply, though, was harsh and unyielding. In essence, the message was, *Keep out of this. It's none of your business.* He would have nothing to do with any scheme which seemed designed to help Phil.

Phil and Israel flew home, with Phil no closer to knowing what he was going to do about Sandy and their unborn child. He had plenty of time to think on the long flights from New York to Christchurch, and he kept coming back to what he knew for certain: Sandy wanted to be with her children, she loved them and she loved him. He would have to give her another chance and that meant rescuing her yet again. This time, he might not be so lucky but he was determined to try.

He had wanted to keep the Hutterites neutral and allow them to act as mediators between Neville and himself, but the response from Neville put an end to that hope. He decided that if he could get Sandy out, he would take up the offer from the Hutterites to take his family to America and live with them.

The biggest problem was how to abduct Sandy for the third time. When he got home, he wasn't surprised to discover from people who had contact with the community that Neville had changed her room yet again, and that he wasn't letting her go into town. He was being extremely careful.

Phil felt powerless. Time was racing by and if Sandy's pregnancy was too far advanced, she wouldn't be allowed to fly. He had to urgently come up with a plan to get her out. He dreamed up hundreds, and discarded them all as too risky. In the end he kept it as simple as possible: he would go in during daylight and grab her. He did the planning and wrote the lists:

- *ask Faith to look after the kids*
- *ask brothers David and Michael to help with kidnap*
- *arrange for friend to drive getaway car*
- *arrange another friend to drive van to community for Phil and brother to hide in*
- *hire two-way radios*
- *arrange for provisions at bach*
- *arrange to have boat waiting*
- *get multiple visa and passport forms to take to bach*
- *get doctor's certificate to say that Sandy is allowed to fly*
- *sell all possessions*

In the second week of December, with the plans in place, it was time to act. Michael went out to the community in advance and hid in the trees across the road from the day-care centre where Sandy worked. He called up on the two-way radio: 'She's in there. Grab her now.'

But Phil and the others were still about 40 minutes away, with David and Phil lying on a mattress in the back of the van Phil's friend Mark was driving. They stopped outside the day-care centre, Mark got out, raised the bonnet and pretended to work on the engine. Ray, the second friend, drove into the community driveway, and went into the day-care centre on the pretext of asking for directions. He didn't know Sandy, and carried a small photo of her concealed in his hand so that he could identify her. When he drove out, he signalled to Mark that she was inside. Ray's part was over and he drove away.

Phil and David leapt out of the van and raced into the day-care centre, but Sandy had gone. Phil knew which route she would have taken so the two of them tore through the screaming children and women, out the door, and caught up with her between the buildings. They grabbed her, but it was too dangerous to take her back the way they had come now that the alarm was raised. They hustled her out to the side road, and there was Ray who had decided to wait around. They bundled Sandy inside his car and were off, with the adrenalin pumping. It had all taken no more than two or three minutes. They were safe, but Mark who was waiting for them outside the buildings with the van got into trouble with the men.

The abduction was caught on camera because one of the television networks got wind of the plan and had cameras waiting. Phil suspects they were tipped off by a former community member with whom Phil had discussed his plans. This man wanted to expose what was happening inside the community and would have seen the abduction as an opportunity to get some publicity. Phil was angry at the time but he is now grateful because although Sandy says she didn't want to go and that she dragged her feet, on film she is not dragging her feet.

At the time, he saw nothing wrong in what he did. His vision was to save her and give her children back to her. He wanted to give them back to their mother, not to the community. They went to Faith's house to pick them up. This time Sandy kept herself emotionally distant from them.

Phil drove his family up to the Sounds, knowing that it was going to be much harder than last time, with Sandy now more indoctrinated than previously, and even stronger in her belief that heaven would only be hers for eternity if she lived in the community. Apparently Neville had increased the pressure by telling her that God required this sacrifice of her. It was God testing her, and she must make the sacrifice of giving up her children so that both she and they would be assured of heaven ever after.

They arrived at the Sounds where the boat was waiting to take them out to the bach. For Phil it was very much déjà vu, except that this time, Sandy was seven and a half months pregnant, he was planning to take her out of the country, she didn't have a passport, and he knew she would refuse to sign the papers to allow him to get one for her. More problems to solve.

David came with them, acting as Phil's security. The eight of them settled into life at the bach, although Phil told David that if he saw a suspicious-looking boat coming, he was to get the shotgun and shoot below the waterline as a warning. He was so focussed on his goal of saving his family that shooting at anyone tying up at the jetty seemed the obvious and right thing to do, since it was likely that Sandy had described to Neville where the bach was. Phil's fear of a raid by Neville was so acute that David slept outside, lying on one of the steps leading up to the bach.

Phil woke early the morning after their arrival to find that Sandy was missing. He tore out of the bach, saw David still asleep with the gun untouched beside him, then he saw Sandy. She was wading out into the bay, her long dress billowing around her as she went. The two men dived in after her, grabbed and pulled her back to shore.

It broke Phil's heart. She was nearly eight months pregnant, and although she was a strong swimmer, she couldn't possibly have swum far enough to find a phone and ring the community. The noise had woken the children and Phil stood back, hoping their love would help her settle. She tended to them, but he could see that she was still keeping the emotional barrier up. Worse was to come. She refused to eat. He didn't know if she was so traumatised that she couldn't, or whether she was choosing not to. Her pain, though, was real. She wanted to be with the children, was desperate to be their mother, but by now she had had a further six months of Neville's conditioning. She was torn, distraught at being once again catapulted into the outside world against her will.

The day passed, and the next, but still she didn't eat. Phil decided she would have to see a doctor, but taking her in to Picton would be too dangerous. He rang the television company who had filmed the abduction and explained the situation to them. They hired a helicopter and flew in a doctor who gave Sandy some medication. It seemed to do the trick; either that, or the chat with the doctor had reassured her. She began eating again and Phil felt it was safe to continue with the organisation required to take his family out of the country.

The passport and visas were the next problem to solve. Phil secretly peeled off the stickers from the visa forms, sat the kids at the table and organised them into a game of practising their signatures. They wanted their mother to join in, which she did. That gave him her signature. He got the camera, took everyone outside and clowned around, managing to get a suitable head shot of Sandy.

David took the film, and the passport application with Sandy's signature stuck on it, to Wellington for processing, while Phil figured out a plan to get them all to Auckland where they would catch a flight to the States. Money to pay for the trip wasn't a problem as he'd sold all their belongings, including the boat. The problem was going to be getting to Auckland without Neville discovering where they were. It was a toss-up between taking the ferry to Wellington and flying to Auckland from there, or driving the whole way, a trip of over 600 kilometres which could well take ten hours. Either scheme was fraught with danger because the longer they were in the public eye, the more likely Neville would be to discover their whereabouts. Phil was certain his father would have hired investigators who wouldn't have any trouble finding them once they were on the road.

So far, though, luck seemed to be on Phil's side. Thanks to help from a friend who was an MP, Sandy's passport was processed overnight, and by mid-afternoon the following day, Phil had it in his hand. It was a huge relief to have cleared the first hurdle. He was still undecided over the best method of getting them all safely to Auckland Airport when he got a phone call that evening. The anonymous caller explained that he'd heard the story of how Phil was trying to keep his family together, and he wanted to help. 'Be at Blenheim Airport tomorrow morning where a plane will be waiting to take you to Auckland Airport. There are seats reserved for you all on a flight to Los Angeles.' He told Phil what time to be at Blenheim Airport, and ended the conversation.

There was such a sense of things happening beyond his control for the good of his family that Phil accepted with gratitude and without question. He rang the Hutterites to say they were on their way.

There was no time for questions, nor to wonder who the mystery benefactor was. Phil told Sandy and the children to pack everything up, but didn't tell them where they were going.

The weather broke overnight so that the family woke to rain blasting sideways on a nor'westerly gale. They struggled down to the jetty with their gear, Sandy trying to keep her balance as she carried Crystal. It was a rough trip to Waikawa Bay and by the time they arrived they were running late. Phil hustled his family into the car then ran to help David with the last of the luggage. Would the plane wait for them? Would it even take off in this weather? There was no time to worry. David jumped into the driver's seat and they were off, with him driving fast, trying to claw back some of the lost time.

The children were asking, *Where are we going? What's happening this time? Is Uncle David coming too?* But they weren't worried; Mum and Dad were both with them, and Dad was in that hyped-up mood where everything was fun and exciting.

The airport was deserted apart from a ten-seater twin-engine plane emblazoned with the Christian Aviation logo, that was waiting on the tarmac where it rocked in the wind. David drove as close as he could but the three adults still had to hold onto the children for the short distance as the wind ripped at them, knocking them sideways. Sandy shepherded her children down the aisle and buckled them in while David and Phil threw the luggage on board.

The children waved back as David said goodbye, before he disappeared out the door for the last time. Their dad grinned at them. 'What an adventure, kids! Your first flight. Except for you, Israel. You can tell your sisters what's going to happen.'

Up front, the pilot turned around to give them a smile while the co-pilot did a quick check to make sure everyone was buckled in correctly. 'We're going to have a few bumps, but don't worry. We'll be perfectly safe.'

They took off. A few bumps! The wind caught the plane, tipping it sideways, then it dropped, rose, and lurched its way up to the cruising altitude. Israel hung on, listening to his mother praying behind him, her voice high. Would God look after them, or would they be blown out of the sky and fall on the ground? This wasn't like the other flights he'd been on, but those planes had been much bigger. This one felt so tiny – it kept falling and tipping as the wind tried to smash it to bits. Somebody was crying. Mum kept praying the whole way. In front of him, though, was Dad's solid figure, and every now and again he'd turn around to grin at them all. Even so, Israel wished they'd hurry up and get to Auckland. He didn't know where they were going after that, but it had to be better than this.

Phil scarcely noticed that they were being thrown around the sky. For him the entire episode had a feeling of unreality. Their escape from Neville was meant to be, and a bit of rough weather wasn't going to stop it.

Finally their plane landed in Auckland where Sandy thanked God for their deliverance. The pilot radioed one of the airport police officers, a fellow Christian, to come and meet them, then he and the co-pilot helped the family gather their belongings and disembark. Phil, carrying Crystal, helped a wobbly Sandy down the steps behind the children. He held Crystal with one arm and Sandy with the other as the police officer ushered them through the airport. The kids stopped inside the doors. 'Dad! They're calling our name! They're talking about the Cooper family!'

They were right. The Cooper family were required to board their aircraft immediately. Phil's heart sank. They were never going to get through immigration in time, especially if Sandy said she was being taken out of the country against her will, or if Neville had discovered what was happening and alerted the authorities. Their name boomed again over the speaker.

However, instead of taking them to immigration, the police

officer led them through a side door, and out over the tarmac to the waiting plane. Phil entered last, glancing behind him, fully expecting to see his father charging towards him. He helped Sandy and the children settle into their seats, all the time looking at the door, waiting for the moment when Neville would appear. Even when the plane began to move, he couldn't relax. Once they were in the air, he slumped back in his seat, closed his eyes, and slept all the way to Los Angeles. The strain of the past weeks had finally hit him. Sandy tended to her children and kept her feelings to herself.

The whole episode later merged into a blur for Phil: the tight schedule, the trip from Blenheim coming so unexpectedly, and the clandestine departure from Auckland without getting their passports checked or stamped. After a stopover in Los Angeles, they flew to New York where they were met by members of the Woodcrest community. Woodcrest, the founding community of the American Bruderhof Hutterites, was in upper New York State, two hours out of New York City. They welcomed the family wholeheartedly. Three days before Christmas was a magical time to arrive; it was snowing and the entire country seemed to be sparkling with lights and bright with decorations.

Quarters had been prepared for the family. They walked in and stared in amazement at the eight Christmas trees – a small one for each member of the family and a big one for all of them. Sandy had to explain Christmas to the children since none of them had ever experienced the pagan celebration in Neville's community. Neither had Phil, but until she was 16 Sandy had lived in the world, with typically worldly Christmases. The children were entranced.

The best was yet to come. On Christmas Day the Coopers joined the whole community in the big dining hall where there were tables set up for each family. They found the one with their name on it – piled high with parcels wrapped in colourful paper. There were gifts for each of them, piles of gifts. The children overcame their awe and began unwrapping the first presents they'd received in their lives: hand-crafted toys and clothing, colouring pencils, scented soap, lollies and biscuits. All around them other families tore paper from their own presents. Phil looked around the room, at the laughing people, the big Christmas tree and the decorations. *Wow! If this is a pagan celebration, give me more!*

For the children, Christmas set the tone for their years in America. Along with the months in the Sounds, it was the happiest time of their childhood. Sandy hadn't been able to keep them at an emotional distance for long, and she soon thawed towards Phil, too. They had a loving, supportive community around them and they were a proper family again, strengthened by relatives making the journey from New Zealand to visit them. Faith and Alan came; so did Wes and Ellen who had been so kind in giving them the use of their bach. Sandy's father Judah came and stayed for some time. It was special for the children to have their grandfather with them.

The children felt as if they'd arrived on a peaceful shore after all the turmoil and upset they'd gone through in New Zealand. For Israel, Woodcrest was like all the good bits in the New Zealand community with none of the bad. It was what Neville's community could have been like.

Phil hoped that living in a strong and Godly community would give Sandy the strength to stay away from Neville and his beliefs. There were similarities between the two communities because the New Zealand one had taken its founding principles from the Hutterites, adopting the modest dress and the God-centred mode of life. The Hutterites celebrated their faith in joyous worship whereas in Neville's community life was starker, with Christmas, Easter, birthdays, the names of the weekdays and the months all forbidden because of their pagan origins. By now Phil's own faith was shaky, and although he went through the motions of worship, he was very cautious about God and he didn't want any involvement. Gradually though, the simple strength of the Hutterite faith impressed him. He couldn't get over the fact that they released their children into the world with their blessing. If they chose to come back – which most of them did – then that was good, but if they didn't, they were still members of the family and could visit freely or be visited out in the world. He found it almost unbelievable that children who had rejected their father's faith would still be loved and accepted members of the family. This was unconditional love in action, something of which he'd had little experience.

The children settled into school and Phil went to work in the workshop where the community manufactured equipment for the disabled.

Sandy's baby was almost due, and she appeared to be adjusting. She and Phil talked about why he'd abducted her yet again, and again he told her he wanted them to be a family. He asked her to give him six months and then if she still wanted to go back, he wouldn't make any more attempts to take her away. He was confident she would stay with them; everything was set up for success and the longer she was away from his father, the stronger she would become.

The baby was born on February 6 1991, and they named him Andreas after the Hutterite elder who had taken the family under his wing. Two months after his birth, the family had to pack up and drive across the border into Canada, apply for new visas, and wait till they came through. They lived with Hutterites in Manitoba for about three months, and when Phil saw that the small communities were struggling to make a living at farming, he set up a workshop and taught them to make waterbeds, which, as far as he knows, they have continued to do.

The children relaxed, revelling in having their family whole and happy again. There was a sense that their family was re-forming, particularly when Judah came to stay with them. But the home videos Phil made of their days in America show Sandy almost always wearing the blue dress from New Zealand. She had long dresses given to her by the Hutterite women, but these were patterned and weren't quite as long as her blue dress. She never wore them unless she had to. On video, she holds herself somewhat aloof during a riotous sports day where all the community are gathered and play games. Bearded, dignified men play catch with water-filled balloons which always burst to soak the catcher. Everyone cheers and there is much laughter. Women form teams for a nail-hammering competition. Adults and children pair up for a game that involves rushing from one side of the big circle of participants to the other. Toddlers wander around and are picked up for a cuddle or comfort by the nearest adult. Everybody participates, or watches laughing from the sidelines. Sandy smiles and responds only when somebody approaches her directly.

Although Tendy was only five when the family arrived in the States, she remembers the fun of the concerts they took part in, and she recalls Israel and Dawn singing at a wedding. The big spring and winter carnivals were exciting, especially the winter ones where they made igloos out of the snow. She can remember silly things, too, like getting caught for stealing her dad's secret stash of liquorice which he kept in a cupboard. When the kids came home from school at lunchtime, they would wash their hands, but before going to the communal dining room, they'd climb up and sneak the liquorice. Tendy put hers in her dress pocket but one day it fell out and the man who was serving came over to tell her she'd dropped it. Busted! Phil sent her back to their quarters without her lunch. She remembers walking out of the big room with all the families sitting together on long benches at the tables, watching her go. But her happiest memories are of living with the Hutterites in America and Canada.

All the children were settled and happy, spring had come, and the countryside was beautiful. There were school expeditions to lakes, picnics in the sun, and an overnight camping trip with singing around the campfire as the sun went down.

But Sandy was struggling. The children have memories of hearing her crying at night after they were in bed. At one point during the months in Canada Phil realised he didn't have her passport. She had hidden it from him and now he suspects that there was a plan afoot to take her back to New Zealand. He believes she must have made the decision to return just before they left Canada because, as she'd done in Christchurch before she left him, she asked him to make love to her. He'd been out working all day and got home to find the children organised and ready for bed. She'd put on the prettiest of her Hutterite dresses and once the children were asleep the two of them went to bed. It was a night of passionate intensity and all he could think was that at last, this was his wife, the real Sandy. It was a unique night in their lives.

But only two or three weeks after the family returned from Canada, she disappeared for an entire day. Phil and others searched the community for her but then he thought to check what she might have taken with her. The only thing missing was her passport. He was terrified for her safety. Why hadn't she talked to him, asked him to let her go home? He had given his word that he'd let her go home after six months if she still wanted to, and she must have known he would keep that promise. He never found out where she went, but assumes it was New York City and she was so inexperienced in the ways of the world that anything could have befallen her. She came back that night, but she was in a deeply distressed state. He knew this was the end. It was a bitter realisation – but she was married to two men, and she had chosen his father. Neville had finally won.

Phil talked to the Hutterite elders, asking them what he should do. They talked to Sandy as well and, in the end, they all saw that she would have to return to New Zealand. The Hutterites bought her a ticket and all that was left was for her to say goodbye to her children.

She spent the night before she left holding Andreas and sobbing, 'My baby. How can I leave my baby?'

Israel, Justine and Tendy all remember the day she left, although the girls were too young to realise that she was going forever. Phil came to the school, called the children out of class and told them their mother was leaving. She'd come and gone before so they just thought she was going away on a little trip.

Israel tried to reassure himself but when he saw that she was crying and he saw the look on his dad's face, he worked out that this time she wasn't coming back. He didn't cry; his dad had always impressed on him that he must be brave for the little ones and he didn't want to start them crying. He remembers his mother telling him as she said goodbye, 'Now Israel, be good to your brother and sisters and really look after them.' He told her he would but he didn't ask her why she was going. He thinks now that he probably knew because he had enough knowledge of Neville's community which would have been telling her, *It's God testing you. You have to give up your children but you'll be reunited in the end.*

They would have used biblical examples: *Isaac was ready to kill his son, and you just have to give your children up for a time.*

The children have seen her since, but that was the last day she was their mother. That day feels sadder to them now than it did then.

She left them a card in which she'd written a short letter. It must have been almost impossible to write and there's a sense in it of her powerlessness. She is powerless to stay with them, and because they are so young she can't give them true understanding of why she is forced to leave them. It's a loving letter and the only way she knew to make sure they would survive without her.

I know there is so much you don't understand and I cannot explain, but please believe that I want to be with you to wipe away your precious tears.

She writes personal messages to each of them:

Israel, love and care for your sisters and brother, be someone they can look up to.

Dawn, be a loving, caring big sister and remember I love you.

Justine and Tender-Joy, love and share with one another and do what the older ones tell you.

There were messages, too, for Crystal and baby Andreas. Seven months after their arrival in America, Phil drove Sandy back to the airport. They barely spoke during the two-hour trip. There was nothing to say, and there was too much to say. He went with her to the check-in counter, all the time hoping she would change her mind. After she'd collected her ticket he helped her find the departure area where he would have to leave her. She hugged him, holding him tight before she said goodbye. He stood watching her walk away down the long corridor. She was torn, he knew that – but the tragedy of it was that they both wanted the same thing. They loved each other and they loved their kids. It should have been simple enough to be together as a family. She turned around three times to wave to him. He felt he must wake soon out of this dream and she'd be there, hugging him. Each time she turned around to wave, he was certain she was going to come back, but she didn't. She vanished around the corner and he stood where he was, crying.

CHAPTER TEN: SOME ANSWERS

The Hutterites were amazing and I don't think my dad or any of us could have got through that time without them and the support they gave us. ISRAEL

The family were shattered, but the decision Sandy felt she had to make almost cost her her life. When she got back home to Neville's community, she was so emotionally distraught that she was unable to eat, and finally they had to seek medical intervention to save her life.

It turned out that Neville had managed to discover that Phil had taken his family to North America and would have known they'd need to cross the US/Canadian border when their visas needed renewing. He ordered Sandy's mother Naomi to contact the Canadian police to tell them her daughter had been abducted from New Zealand against her will. Neville knew the strength of Sandy's love for her children, so his hope was that the decision to return would be taken out of her hands by the authorities.

Naomi had done as the hierarchy told her, also phoning Sandy constantly to persuade her to return. She was happy enough to do so, believing that Phil would come back, too. Later, she had a hard time forgiving herself for the devastation she'd helped cause.

Naomi would later tell Phil of a phone conversation where Sandy said she wasn't sure she wanted to return. He reckons the fact that she didn't ever alert the border authorities shows her ambivalence. Each time they had to cross between countries he was on edge, knowing she could tell them at any point, but he realised, too, that she was in an invidious position. How could she tell them she wanted to leave the country and leave her children behind?

But now Sandy had left her family behind forever, and the Hutterites surrounded them with love, involving them in activities to keep them distracted and busy. A couple from the Catskills community in upper state New York offered to become their surrogate parents. Phil accepted gratefully, even though it meant moving from Woodcrest. The Catskills couple more or less adopted them, helped Phil with the children, and provided them all with a loving, stable environment. Israel describes them as a blessing and the security they provided freed him from the stomach pains that came whenever he was stressed.

In the months after Sandy's departure, Phil concentrated on being the best dad he could be. He still hoped against hope that Sandy would come back, but in any case he didn't want the children to forget her. Every day after they'd finished their homework, he got them to write her letters or draw a picture. He posted them off regularly, including work they'd done at school. To keep her in touch with Andreas, he made hand and foot prints by standing him in paint when he was eighteen months old. He cut off a lock of Andreas's hair, so white it barely showed up on the paper, and sent that with the children's letters. Crystal's bedtime stories every night were those he told her about her mother. They'd sit together in her bed, looking at photograph albums while he told her the stories.

He stood Sandy's photo on a wooden plaque in the shape of

praying hands, with a message on its base: *Dear God, please bring Mummy back*. That photo and the message accompanied them to house after house in the years to come. Every day he got the children to write to their mother and pray to God to bring her back. He wanted to give them something to believe in, to give them hope, but also to make sure they didn't ever feel bitter at her for leaving them.

Not long after Sandy left, Andreas who was six months old developed a bad case of reflux that deteriorated over the following year to the stage where he had trouble breathing and wasn't able to eat. He had surgery at 18 months old and had to be fed through a tube directly into his stomach. Israel had taken him under his wing, looking after his young brother as his mother had asked him to, and any anger he felt over her leaving was on his brother's behalf: 'He was only eighteen months old and he had to go into major surgery and it had to have resulted from the stress of Mum leaving like that – just gone.'

The loving support of the Hutterite community made the blow of their mother's departure bearable for the older children. Life was good, there was plenty to do, lots of friends to play with, and always an 'aunt' or their surrogate mother to go to when they wanted a motherly presence. It was ideal for Phil, too; he had the support of the whole community, but he was more responsible for his children's daily care than he'd been able to be in New Zealand. His family had their own accommodation; help was available if he needed it, and he was living in a community structured around the care of its families. It was his learning time in how to be a parent.

In June 1993 Phil flew home to New Zealand to prepare for the fraud trial Clive Bilbie had brought against the community. While over there, he went down to Christchurch to visit family and talk to Faith who had been growing increasingly worried about the abuse going on in the community. She had taken in too many people Neville had abused, and wanted it to stop.

Neville's leadership of his community gave him total power in any situation regarding his followers. He was free to manipulate, abuse and control anyone as he chose. There was no redress inside the community, nowhere to turn and nobody who could help. His demand for silence from his victims meant that they couldn't begin to try to find an advocate. The mind-control was all pervasive and all but impossible to withstand, especially by young women who had been children when their parents joined Neville's Church at Springbank.

Faith and Phil abhorred the sexual abuse, the mind control, and the way their father had of breaking families apart. They gathered together a group of those affected. The group talked it over and decided to go out to the community, talk to Neville, and ask him for an apology. All they wanted was for him to say yes, he'd done wrong and he was sorry. They hoped to make him aware that the outside world would never condone his actions, and that he would choose to desist from further abuse. This would also give some peace of mind to those struggling as a result of his actions.

There were other abusers besides Neville in the community, and Phil tried to persuade a young man who had suffered badly at the hands of one of the men to join the group. The young man refused; he couldn't bear to think about it, let alone expose to the world what he saw as his own shame. He couldn't believe in Phil's assurances that the shame wasn't his, but the other man's.

Phil and ten former members drove to the community to talk to Neville. He refused to have anything to do with them. They had betrayed him by leaving and he was adamant that he himself had done nothing he needed to apologise for. He would not speak to them.

This wasn't the result any of them had hoped for and it left them with the problem of what to do next. After much thought, they decided to go to the police and lay charges.

The Christchurch police began an investigation at the end of June 1993. In July Phil went back to Wellington for the fraud trial, to be met at Wellington Airport by a barrage of media because two days previously, on July 20, police had conducted simultaneous dawn raids on the community premises at Springbank and at their new location on the West Coast. Neville had been arrested. The two raids were necessary because some of Neville's community were now living on the West Coast while others remained to wind up affairs at Springbank. The new property, inland from Greymouth in the South Island of New Zealand, was bigger and much more isolated. The community had bought 917 hectares of land, possibly using money from inheritances to do so (and later would buy an adjoining block so that they currently own a total of 1700 hectares). Since 1991 when they bought the land they had been preparing it to be their headquarters, building the milking sheds first and then the accommodation blocks for the people. Gloria had died in March 1991 during the setting up phase of the new community and Neville named it Gloriavale in her honour.

The raids shook the community to its foundations. The arrest of the leader of the Cooperite sect (as they were popularly known) for sexual violation made headline news around the country, hence the media interest in Phil's presence in Wellington.

The fraud trial went ahead. Phil enjoyed the judge's questioning of Neville who now went by the name of Hopeful Christian:

'Is there a Fervent Stedfast in the community?'

'Yes.'

'Is there a Hopeful Christian in the community?'

'Yes.'

'Is there an honest Christian in the community?'

'No.'

The community was found guilty and ordered to pay reparation of $140,000.

Phil flew back to America and made the decision to leave the shelter of the Hutterite communities in order to strike out on his own. The children would have been happy to stay forever, but he was wanting a wider world once again, where he could do things his way. This community was a loving and truly Godly one, but Phil wanted to be fully in charge of his own life. At the end of September 1993, not quite three years after they'd arrived, he packed up his family for another adventure.

He decided not to return to New Zealand. He was an Australian citizen so he would take his children there, find a small town by the sea, and make a life for them all. He chose Coffs Harbour, remembering it from the holiday Neville had taken him on when he was a teenager.

He told the children they were going to leave America, but it would be a huge adventure because they were going to live in Australia. They were excited because Sandy had told them stories about the kangaroo that used to steal the bread when she was a child there, and now they would see a real kangaroo. Israel was torn: he was excited about the adventure but he hated the thought of leaving all their friends. The stomach pains hit again, and again he kept them to himself.

The Hutterites bought their tickets, farewelled the family, and gave Phil about $4,000 to tide him over. Although Phil had willingly contributed his labour and expertise to their workforce, he was still humbled by their generosity. Their attitude and assistance were so different from anything he'd experienced from his own father.

The departure wasn't straightforward because Andreas was an American citizen and needed his mother's signature on his visa to get into Australia. Phil decided to chance his luck. At the airport in New York, he put their seven passports together, with Andreas's at the bottom, took them up to the check-in counter, waited till the woman was about to check Andreas's, then made a comment to one of the kids which was enough to distract her. She smiled at them all, handed back the passports, and they were through.

The hearts of fellow passengers must have sunk when they saw this man with his six young children board the plane for the long flights, but at the end of each leg people came up to him and told him how wonderful the children had been and congratulated him on his family.

Immigration in Sydney detained Phil because of Andreas's status, but he'd been right in gambling on the fact that they wouldn't send a toddler back by himself. They let him in and gave Phil 24 days to sort it out. He would immediately apply for Andreas's Australian citizenship.

Once they got through immigration, Israel took charge, telling his dad that he'd look after the others while Phil went to buy bus tickets to Coffs Harbour. Phil had arranged for the friend they'd stayed with in Coffs when he was a teenager to meet them. He hoped the friend would have found accommodation for them – somewhere they could live, where their lack of possessions wouldn't be too much of a handicap. Their only belongings were those they carried in their ten pieces of luggage.

The friend picked them up from the bus station, took them to a one-roomed flat attached to a church, where they could stay, then he took Phil to the welfare office to see what government support he might be entitled to.

CHAPTER ELEVEN:
LIFE IN A NEW COUNTRY

So we picked up and moved to Australia and started afresh.
It was there that the reality hit that Mum wasn't coming back.
There was a huge void. I really felt it and that's when I missed her.
I remember Dawn and Tendy crying. That's the first time
I cried because I missed my mum. ISRAEL

In Australia the full impact of Sandy's departure hit the family. Now that they were alone in the outside world they felt her absence sharply. The worst thing was having to accept that she was gone forever. Phil had to acknowledge that his father had won; there would be no more attempts to take her out. He threw his energies into proving to Neville that he could make it on the outside, that he could create a good life for his children – and he was utterly determined to be a far better father than Neville was.

They struggled financially and emotionally. Until now there had always been a community or family to help but suddenly they were on their own. Phil didn't have the resources to pay for counselling for the children, had he even thought of it. His father's community believed sickness to be a weakness, and emotional distress sheer self-indulgence (although they had sought help for

Sandy when her distress looked to be endangering her life). Phil had no precedence for seeking emotional help; he didn't know such a thing was available and didn't recognise that his children could be helped by outside assistance. In America, the Hutterites had well organised systems for dealing with illness, but they were far away and the children weren't physically ill.

Phil had to learn how to be a father and a mother to his children, while they had to try and adjust to the loneliness of a life where it was just the six of them and their dad. The parenting skills Phil had learnt from the Hutterites were invaluable, but nothing could have prepared him for coping with children who cried for their mother every night. He felt pulled in two directions; his kids needed him but he also needed to earn money which he couldn't do if he stayed at home with them. The hardest thing, though, was not being able to tell them he'd get their mother back. She was gone and she'd left them of her own accord.

For several weeks after they arrived, the children couldn't sleep alone and would squash together into Phil's double bed and cry for their mother. Without the happy distractions of community life, they keenly felt the reality that she wasn't just across town; she was in another country and another world. Their dad couldn't drive off in the night and get her. When Phil found a house to rent, they still climbed into each other's beds to alleviate the loneliness. One or other of them would wake in the night, crying because they'd wet the bed. Phil would take them into his bed and sometimes they would wet that as well. It was several years before they could all sleep by themselves in their own beds.

Dawn, especially, missed her mother, and for a long time, she would cry at night. Justine and Tendy, who shared a room with her, didn't entirely understand why she was crying but they would join in. Phil did his best to comfort and distract them. During daylight, things were better although it was months before Dawn was happy again and even then her dad would glimpse the sadness that was never far from the surface.

Israel's stomach pains were bad, but he still didn't tell his father.

For the first few weeks Phil didn't attempt to send the children to school. Eleven-year-old Israel looked after Andreas and his sisters while their dad worked at anything he could find. Sandy had always impressed on her son that the most important thing for an older brother was to look after his brother and sisters and he saw it as natural to step up and take care of them. He expanded his cooking repertoire and taught himself to make proper meals. He taught himself and his siblings to do the washing and the cleaning. All the children pitched in with their chores, but Israel was the one who took on the responsibility for running the house and looking after the others. He was a fastidious cook and housekeeper and taught the others the right way of doing things. He believes now that Sandy knew she wasn't going to be with her children and that she was doing her best to protect them as much as she could when she told Israel to look after them.

Money was tight, even though the welfare benefit was far more than Phil had hoped for, and he also got assistance to pay the electricity bill, received food vouchers, and sometimes baskets of provisions as well. The children would fall on the baskets. What was inside? Usually there was some item that was a huge treat, such as a bar of chocolate, or a packet of biscuits, and one red-letter day, a packet of crisps.

The trouble was that they were starting from nothing, with every piece of furniture, replacement clothing, and household equipment needing to be bought. It was never easy finding a place to rent: not many landlords wanted a single dad with six kids for a tenant.

Life was tough, but Phil vowed again that life in Australia would be fun for his kids, that they would have a better father and a better life than he had had. He was determined, too, that they would prosper. He managed the money in every way he could. In October of 1993, a month after their rented house had been sold out from under them, they moved into a caravan park where they lived until the new year in a basic, two-roomed cabin. The kids loved it: it was practically on the beach, they were happy being close together in the small space and, best of all, their dad spent a lot of time with them. He rigged up an ancient black and white television set he'd got hold of for next to nothing and they'd rent ten movies for ten dollars. Israel was entranced. The movies taught him much about the world that he hadn't known. He loved immersing himself in these vivid stories that always ended happily. In a movie you could make a fairytale ending happen. When he grew up, he decided, he would make movies and they would always end happily ever after.

In November the family received an invitation to the Channel 10 Christmas party. They couldn't believe it – a real Christmas party! They looked forward to it for weeks, talking about what it might be like but they had nothing to base their speculation on because neither of the communities they'd lived in had ever had what they called a party. Perhaps it would be like the Hutterite Christmas celebrations, with presents, music, carols and streamers. At last the day came; they dressed up in their best clothes and set out for the first party of their lives. Phil was just as excited as his kids.

They arrived and stopped still in the doorway so that Phil had to usher them inside. This was beyond their expectations. They'd never imagined so much colour, so many decorations, a tree with flashing lights and enticingly wrapped presents heaped at its base. They stared, shocked at such an excess of riches.

Clowns danced, fairies twirled, stilt-walkers teetered and balloons floated on the ceiling. The family stood still, too afraid to touch anything.

Then Santa Claus arrived. He picked up presents from the big pile and handed them out. He called Israel's name. Then Dawn's. Gradually the children realised they were all getting presents from this strangely dressed man. They looked at Phil, checking that it was okay before they tore off the wrapping paper. Israel's present was a helicopter. Dawn's a pink brush and comb with a mirror set with sparkling stones. Each present was magical; the day itself was magical with a feeling of unreality. Maybe it wasn't real. Maybe they were inside a movie.

Phil loved the whole thing. The production aspect of it especially appealed to him, but he was shocked to discover that the party was for underprivileged kids, and that his kids were so considered. If he'd known that, he probably wouldn't have taken them, because to him they weren't underprivileged, they simply had problems to solve. But that party turned out to be such a highlight in their lives that now he donates money to it every year.

By Christmas the family were still living in the caravan park. On Christmas Eve, Phil went off to bed, leaving them to sit up and watch a movie called *A Mom for Christmas* in which an 11-year-old girl whose mother died when she was young gets her wish for a new mother. It was a poignant movie; the girls were in tears before it was very far through but all six watched avidly till the end. They went to sleep hoping to wake up in the morning to find their mum had come back, hoping for their own fairytale ending.

They moved house a lot in those first years, but in every house Phil would put the photo of Sandy in the lounge. He didn't want the children to forget their mother, and he worked to keep a connection by encouraging them to write to her, even though she never replied. They were devastated years later when rummaging in a cupboard at home, to come across all their letters, unopened and marked *Return to Sender.* It was a while before they realised it had probably been their grandfather's doing and that their father had hidden the letters because he didn't want them to know their mother hadn't received them. In fact, Phil had been devastated when the hundreds of letters were all returned from the community in a big bag. After a lot of thought, he decided not to tell the children, but to get them to keep writing and keep believing their mum was getting their letters.

Phil created distractions: he wanted to make the adventure he'd promised them come true; he wanted to give them a bigger life and he didn't want them to dwell on losing their mother. He wanted to give them the kind of fun other children had, while also helping them fit into and understand this strange world he'd brought them to. Spurring him on was the determination that Neville was not going to win this particular battle. Phil would make sure that he had a good relationship with his kids; he would not be like his father.

Typically, the first adventure he took them on was big and fraught with obstacles – or to him, problems to solve. In the new year of 1994 he decided to take them to Cairns to visit their friends Colin and Dawn, a journey of over 1600 kilometres. They were living in the caravan park because they had no money, so flying to

Cairns was out of the question. If they drove they would have to stay several nights on the road. Phil knew these problems could be solved with the right attitude and a bit of ingenuity. He bought an old van with the money from the Hutterites, and to entertain the children during the long days on the road, he bolted the old television on the ceiling of the van, connected it up to a video, and powered it all from the engine battery. The Cooper kids had on-board entertainment before portable gear became available.

They travelled through the heat of the summer up into the tropics in a van with no air-conditioning, the children lying on mattresses and watching videos. At night they slept in camping grounds or at the side of the road. They had no camping gear; it was too hot in the van so they slept outside. The mosquitoes were fierce. They remember it now as a crazy, fun time when they never knew what might happen next. Dad was always there and they were having the huge adventure he'd promised them.

Colin and Dawn welcomed them in Cairns, setting up a campsite for them on their tropical fruit farm. For the children it was bliss to be with a family again, and nine-year-old Dawn was thrilled to meet the woman she had been named after. They stayed through January and February, loving this experience of the exotic Australia they had imagined. There was lots happening, plenty to do, and always in the background a caring, motherly presence.

While they were in Cairns, Phil kept in touch with his family in New Zealand, and heard in late January 1994 that Neville was to appear in the Christchurch District Court for a depositions hearing, to face nine counts of indecent assault involving five complainants who had been between 12 and 19 years old at the time of the alleged offending. Phil was named as one of the complainants.

The trial itself would not take place until December the following year. Phil's feelings were mixed. Yes, his father needed to understand what he had done, but Phil knew, too, the skill with which he could twist things to show himself in the best possible light. He was sorry he wasn't able to be in Christchurch with his siblings for the hearing.

On the drive back to Coffs Harbour at the end of February, Phil stopped to pick up a hitchhiker. Nina was a 19-year-old who worked as a nanny and he employed her as a live-in home help. Having Nina lightened the load all round, but while Israel was glad to have the help, he objected to her taking over and would tell her that he was the one looking after the kids, that he had the responsibility here. She would be an on-and-off presence in their lives for several years, staying a while then taking off travelling again.

Back in Coffs Harbour, with Nina to look after the two little ones, Phil settled the older children into schools. Justine was glad to be back in school where she could play sport. She made friends easily and fitted in but Israel, Dawn and Tendy struggled. Israel was bewildered by these kids who talked of things he knew nothing about; theirs was still an alien world. They'd ask the normal sort of questions like, How come you talk with an American accent? What does your dad do? Does your mum work? It was impossible to explain his history in a few words. Each day at home he'd practise explanations in his head, but it was too hard. He didn't want to explain it either; it was shameful and they wouldn't understand anyway, so he invented stories to make his family sound normal: Yes, he had a mother and a father and yes, they had jobs. He would listen to the other kids talk about their favourite TV programmes and which movie stars they liked – yes, he liked those ones, too. By now the stomach pains were pretty much a constant in his life.

All Israel wanted was to blend in, to be the same as the other kids, but his family situation and history marked him out as different. He avoided school whenever he could, which was easy enough when Nina wasn't around and his father couldn't find babysitters for the two little ones. Israel looked after them, cleaned the house, and cooked the meals. Phil remembers coming home one evening tired and despondent about being the only parent, and Israel telling him, 'Dad, take the kids to the park and I'll cook dinner.'

When they got back, the table was set and Israel was ready to serve the meal. His education suffered; he missed a lot of his final two years at primary school and the first year of high school. One of the things Phil feels guilty about now is that Israel missed out on being a normal teenager. For Crystal and Andreas, Israel was more of a parent than a big brother.

Phil was constantly trying to earn enough money, be the best father he could, and manage the budget so that the kids didn't miss out. Moving house whenever the rent went up, though, sometimes meant living in one of the satellite towns outside Coffs. Justine would eventually tally six primary schools and three high schools that she had attended. She and Tendy went to one high school an hour's bus ride away and she hated it because she couldn't play sport after school.

Phil was driven, determined to make their life work, and to make sure his kids didn't suffer. He was equally determined that they weren't going to grow up feeling deprived or self-pitying, and he planned ways of letting them have treats. About once a month he'd manage to give them each a dollar to spend at the school tuckshop. Those days were highlights.

'What are you going to get?'

'I'm going to get chippies. What about you?'

'I had chippies last time. I'm going to buy lollies.'

'An ice-block! I'm getting an ice-block.'

The Cooper kids were the only ones who never bought their lunches from the tuckshop – they were the ones who sat down with their two marmite sandwiches and a piece of fruit. Tuckshop day was brilliant, a huge treat made all the sweeter by anticipation. It also made them feel that they were like the other kids.

If his kids wanted something more expensive, such as to go to a movie, Phil would sit them down and together they'd work out a way to get the money. He bought bulk supplies of lollies for them to sell on the street, making a competition of it to see who could sell the most. If they wanted to go to Hungry Jack's for hamburgers he'd take them around town to travel agencies who all stocked a free magazine with a 'Buy one, get one free hamburger' voucher in it. He'd send a different kid into each place until they had enough vouchers to provide hamburgers for half the family. He wanted them to see that they could change their world, and that they didn't have to settle for less than they wanted.

He developed the lolly-selling into a business, driving the kids to outlying towns where they would go door-knocking in pairs with their baskets of lollies, selling them for a dollar a packet more than Phil paid for them. He split the profits with them 50/50. He employed other kids, too, whose parents would drive them to the various towns. Phil taught his kids to be entrepreneurial, that there was no such thing as *can't,* and that nothing was out of their reach. He wanted them to see that they could do and achieve anything because there was always a solution. You just had to be prepared to look for it.

The arrest of the leader of the New Zealand religious sect made news across the Tasman and it wasn't long before the media in Australia discovered that one of the complainants was living in Coffs Harbour. When Phil was approached by *60 Minutes Australia* they asked if there was anything they could do for him in exchange for his story, but it didn't occur to him to ask for money. Instead he sent them a list of equipment his family needed. The producers must have been bemused, and gave him a cheque for $10,000 rather than buying the list of items.

Phil had never been afraid of the media and became skilled at marketing his story, to the extent that when the women's magazines started contacting him he had no hesitation about negotiating payment. He was always looking at ways to benefit the children although when he convinced a designer clothing store to provide clothes for them for a year, in exchange for publicity photos of them wearing the clothes, the kids were less than delighted. The outfits were distinctive and didn't help them in their efforts to blend in with their peers.

After the television documentary screened, people kept coming up to him saying how much they pitied him. *Oh, you poor thing*, particularly grated. They weren't poor things. They didn't need anyone's pity. Phil didn't want that and he didn't want the government assistance he was entitled to either because he refused to accept the underprivileged label. He felt strongly that if a *poor me* mentality filtered down to the children, then they were doomed. He wanted them to see that they could create their own opportunities, that this strange new world he had brought them to could become a good place for them.

Phil had to find a way to make money. As on so many other

occasions, he decided he would start by making a plan. Furniture-making and building were what he knew, and with the $10,000 payment from *60 Minutes* he could buy the tools he needed to set himself up. He'd never doubted that he could make money; he'd done it for the community, so he could do it for his family. He regimented the children in order to free up time so he could make furniture in the evenings. Israel cooked and cleaned up the kitchen. Dawn, Justine and Tendy were responsible for putting themselves to bed while Phil bathed Crystal and Andreas, sang them a song, and tucked them up. At nine o'clock Phil started work. He put an ad in the paper the next day and sold what he'd made the night before, making between $50 and $60 each day.

Gradually, the family found they had more money to spend, although the habits of frugality stayed with them.

Back in New Zealand, Melanie Reid of TV3 went undercover to make a documentary of the Cooperite sect as it was still commonly referred to by the public. In May 1994 she rang Phil to tell him she'd just filmed footage inside Gloriavale. She had something to tell him. Would he come to New Zealand? She wanted to film him while she told him, but if when he viewed the footage he didn't want it included, she would honour that. He couldn't imagine what it might be about, but assumed it would be to do with the charges against Neville.

Phil took Dawn with him and they flew to Christchurch.

Melanie's news stunned him.

'You have a seventh child, a daughter. Her name is Cherish and she's two years old.'

He watches that footage now and sees himself sitting there, just repeating what she's said, unable to take it in.

Then the anger kicked in. They had his daughter and they'd

kept her a secret. It was all Neville's doing and Phil wasn't having it. He would go out there right that minute and get her back.

Dawn wanted to see Sandy and her new sister so Phil took her with him. The television crew followed. Looking back, he says it was a dumb thing to do. Neville was never going to let him near Cherish and he had all his community behind him. But the adrenalin was racing and making a plan didn't cross Phil's mind. They arrived at dinner-time when all the community were sitting in the big dining room. He saw Sandy, but Cherish wasn't there, only an empty high chair beside her. Later he learned that Sandy with great presence of mind had pushed Cherish across the table so that she appeared to belong to a different family.

On the film footage Neville jumps up and orders him out. Phil keeps saying that Dawn just wants to see her mother. Neville growls out an order: 'Gather round, men.'

There is more yelling. Fingers stab the air. Eventually Dawn is allowed to see Sandy in her quarters. Phil is hustled outside. A cameraman is punched to the ground. Phil's glasses fall off and are trampled. Some of the crew's equipment is broken.

What wasn't caught on camera was the men chasing the TV crew out of the building where they managed to grab one of the cameramen, bash him up and confiscate his equipment, including the film he'd shot. They chased the other cameraman through bush and paddocks but as he was running he managed to swap the film in the camera for a blank tape he had in his pocket and throw the other one into a fence post hole. When they caught him, he ejected the blank tape and handed it over. They roughed him up even so and chased him off the property.

Retrieving the tape from the post hole was going to be tricky because the community immediately posted guards on the gate.

The next day, after much thought, the crew decided to ask if they could go back to apologise and collect their confiscated gear. The community gave their permission and it was then simply a matter of pausing long enough at the hole to retrieve the tape.

Phil didn't get to see Cherish. He gave Melanie permission to screen the footage.

Undoubtedly he would have been barred from contact anyway, but his involvement in bringing the sex charges against his father ensured that he wasn't going to get anything he asked for.

There's footage of Dawn back in Christchurch afterwards. Still with her American accent, she says, 'The baby wasn't there. Cherish wasn't there.' She can't understand what happened.

When she's asked about her mother not being with them, she says she tries not to think about it. She tells how she sent the community a letter and wrote on it, *I bet you wouldn't like it if you had no mum*. She speaks of her brief visit to Sandy. 'Mum tried to tell me to come back here, and she doesn't want me to go and stay with Dad. She tried to tell me that Dad was a bad person and stuff. But at least she got a photo of us – of all of us.' About Cherish she says, 'They were too scared Dad would just grab the baby and go. I'd rather stay with my mum, but not in that community. I didn't want to leave her.' She says she'd like to get the army and just go in and rescue her and the baby.

Phil had been stunned to find he had a seventh child, but once he cooled down he was forced to accept that she was in the community forever. He discovered later that when Sandy returned from America she hadn't known she was pregnant and was devastated when she found out. She thought Neville would say she was carrying a bastard because of what he'd said when she was pregnant with Andreas, but Neville, no doubt recognising the power the child would give him over Phil, decided that this baby was a blessing.

Cherish's birth certificate gives her date of birth as May 1992. Sandy, by this time, had changed her own name from Sandra Cooper to Prayer Darling. Cherish's surname is registered as Darling, but according to the information on the certificate, she has no father. Sandy says God gave her Cherish, but Phil feels he might have had a bit to do with it himself. He's certain that this daughter was conceived in Canada on the amorous night that Sandy had instigated.

Knowing Phil had discovered Cherish's existence, Neville took extreme precautions. He ordered Naomi and Sandy to keep bags packed with what they called their disguise clothes – clothing that wouldn't look out of place in the outside world. Whenever Phil was in the country, or whenever they heard a rumour that he was there, Neville would give Naomi $1000 and send her, Sandy and Cherish away from Gloriavale for a month. Once, somebody returning from a trip to Greymouth reported that they'd seen Phil. Naomi and Sandy grabbed Cherish and their disguise clothes, jumped in a van, and disappeared for four weeks. Phil hadn't even been in the country.

All this is proof to Phil that the entire saga of his marriage and its subsequent demise is not about him and Sandy; it's about his father and him.

He prepared to return home from Christchurch, his mind still spinning from the news of this seventh child. It was difficult to take in, as was the depth of hate his father harboured for him. It was a hatred born of Neville's own version and interpretation of events, which as far as Phil could see, had no respect for what had really happened.

Phil was relieved to turn his mind to other matters. It was good that his brother Michael had finally agreed to come and live with him and his family in Australia. The kids were also looking forward to seeing Michael. Phil told him how they had his room all ready and couldn't wait for him to get there.

Both brothers had dinner that evening with Faith and her children – Alan was away for the weekend. All of them were cheered to see how much happier and more relaxed Michael was. He tipped the coins out of his pockets and scattered them among his nieces and nephews, teasing them and laughing with them. He was light-hearted and full of fun. Phil hugged him goodbye at the end of the evening, telling him again how great it was going to be, having him come to live with his family. Phil drove back to the friends he was staying with full of hope for Michael.

At around 11 that night Faith was woken by the police knocking on the door. Michael had been found hanging in Linwood Park. She and her son David went with the police to formally identify the body.

Phil stayed on for the funeral. Faith notified the community when the funeral was to be. They responded by saying they would bury Michael next to his mother at Gloriavale. It was ten years since Michael's first expulsion from the community. Neville would bury the son he'd rejected, but only on his own terms. The funeral went ahead in Christchurch, with none of the Gloriavale family in attendance. The burial was included in the TV documentary. Rain falls as the casket is lowered into the earth. The brothers and sisters who tried so hard to support Michael as he struggled with depression and drug abuse weep for the loss of the young man they loved, who had found no way to live happily in the world.

Phil had to go home and break the news to his kids, a task made more difficult by his lack of a partner. On the plane trip home, he felt numb. Michael had been so full of life before his cruel expulsion from the community and now he was dead. Knowing something of the anguish his brother had suffered, Phil was devastated. Later he would feel angry. Right now there was too much grief to leave room for anger.

CHAPTER TWELVE: A REVELATION

Likewise, the husband is bound to the wife as long as she lives, and only if she dies is he loosed from the law of his wife so that he is free to marry another woman.
<small>WHAT WE BELIEVE, P. 57</small>

Phil struggled with being single but never thought of trying to find another partner. Neville's edict had been that only if your spouse died were you free to marry again and Phil never thought to question it. Even though his religious belief had faded away, he'd not examined many of the rules instilled in him as he grew up, including the one concerning divorce. God didn't allow divorce therefore you weren't free to marry again while your spouse lived. However, one day Tendy asked him a question that blew his mind: were they ever going to get a new mother? Once the idea was planted, it took hold. Phil knew nothing about dating or how to build a relationship with a woman but in typical fashion, he charged headlong into the unknown territory of finding a mate.

He decided a dating agency would be the best way of going about it and his first introduction was to Carol, a single mother with one child. He didn't wait for introductions to anyone else, but blasted into her quiet life, catching her up in the energy he created. Despite the obvious 'handicap' of coming as a package with his six children, he impressed her with his vitality and irrepressible spontaneity. They could make this work, of course they could. He swept her along on the tide of his optimism and zest for life. She moved in with her son not long after she and Phil started dating. He assumed the relationship would be permanent and accordingly set about getting a divorce from Sandy. He didn't think it would be easy, but he sent her the papers and was astonished when they came back signed. Perhaps she didn't tell Neville, who would almost certainly have refused any request his son made – especially this one. The family don't know why she signed, and without any fuss. Phil was too grateful to spend much time wondering about it.

Phil's children loved having Carol's motherly presence. They'd had Nina but she was always more like a big sister than a mother. It was great, too, to have Carol's little son as part of the family.

With Carol there to care for the children, Phil put his time and energies into making money. In October 1994 he was able to take Carol, her son, and his kids to the Gold Coast fun parks for a holiday. A home video shot at Sea World shows Phil smiling at the camera, his hands on Carol's shoulders, saying, 'And this is Mrs Cooper.'

She pulls away. 'You wish.'

The relationship had too much stacked against it. They had different expectations of marriage, and Phil's previous experience hadn't prepared him for a partner who wasn't programmed to accept everything he did and said with meek submission. He didn't understand that he needed to put the time into building a solid partnership. Not long after the holiday, it ended badly. Nina also fell out with Phil, sided with Carol over the split, and moved out of Phil's house to live with her.

The children missed Carol, Dawn more than the others. She had never stopped grieving for Sandy and now another mother-figure had left her. Phil was happy for his kids to keep up the relationship, encouraging them to visit whenever they wanted to, and Dawn spent a lot of time with Carol and Nina. Israel remembers Carol trying to play the children off against their father. He'd seen enough of his grandfather's control games to be aware of what she was trying to do and, as he saw it, she was using them to get back at Phil. Dawn's behaviour began to deteriorate and where she led, Justine and Tendy followed.

Phil reacted to the break-up in his usual manner, putting his head down and working. However it wasn't long before he began to think again of finding a partner. He went back to the dating agency and early in 1995 received an introduction to Bev who, like Carol, was a single mother with a young son. For the first few times when Phil went to meet her, he took Crystal and Andreas with him. She assumed that these were the children mentioned on his profile until one day he said he had something to tell her and pulled out a photo of all six children. But that wasn't all. He showed her the magazine articles about them and told her he would understand if she wanted to end the relationship. She decided not to and they kept dating. Her friends and work colleagues were fascinated that she was dating the man whose face they had seen in the magazines, and with whose story they were familiar.

A home video made in April that year has a comment from Bev that might be telling about the relationship. She looks at the camera and says, 'There's Dad, on the mobile like always.' However, Phil's enthusiasm for life, the excitement he created, and the whirl of energy around him won the day, along with his certainty that they could make the relationship work. Bev moved in to his household not long after they started dating. The children were excited when Phil told them Bev and her little son Mitchell were coming to live with them. A new mother! Somebody to look after them.

They dressed in their best clothes to wait for her. Ten-year-old Tendy especially looked forward to having somebody who would give her attention. Maybe with the new mother she'd no longer feel like the odd one out, the middle child with nothing special to recommend her – unlike Justine the other middle child who was tomboyish, sporty and so like their father.

Even though Israel liked having a new mother and therefore a normal family, he realises he must have been a pain in the neck to Bev because he insisted on looking after the others the way he'd always done. He knew how to, and she didn't do things the way he liked them done. He used every excuse he could to stay home because it was still so much easier than going to school, and his stomach didn't hurt so much when he didn't have to face school.

The girls welcomed Bev. It was great to have a mother again and Tendy particularly developed a special bond with her. Andreas got a new brother, a bit younger than he was. All the kids loved having a toddler in the family again.

Bev threw herself into family life. She joined Phil in the lolly-selling business as well as taking on as much of the role of mother as Israel would let her. By this time, as well as having stomach pains, he sometimes had to get up in the night to vomit. He hid it from Bev as well as Phil, experimenting with anything he thought might help. He discovered that eating plain white bread last thing at night was often enough to prevent the vomiting.

Later in the year Sandy's younger sister Yvette who had left the community along with Judah, their father, came to stay. She saw that Israel wasn't well and noticed the way he often pressed his stomach after he'd eaten. When she tackled him about it, he told her about the pains but reassured her he was okay, he'd worked out how to deal with the vomiting. She was horrified and dragged him off to the doctor, something he'd never considered. Doctors cost money and in the back of his mind was the community belief that illness was a sign of weakness so you didn't complain. The doctor prescribed ulcer medication which he had to take for a year. It fixed the pain and vomiting, and the follow-up appointment for an endoscopy a year later clearly showed the scarring from a stomach ulcer.

In December 1995 Phil and Yvette both returned to Christchurch for Neville's trial on 11 counts of sexual violation, one of which was the masturbation of Phil as a teenager. Phil found it an excruciating ordeal, especially when Neville's lawyer tried to go into detail such as the expression on Neville's face, and which hand he had used. Phil just looked over at his father and told the lawyer to ask him, he was the one who knew.

The jury brought in a guilty verdict and Neville was sentenced to five years' imprisonment on ten counts of sexual violation. He appealed and a date was set for the case to be heard in the Court of Appeal in Wellington in May of the following year.

Phil came back from the December trial and threw himself into work, more determined than ever to show his father he could succeed on his own out in the world. He and Bev discussed their future and how they would support their family. Phil, with the experience of the waterbed business behind him and knowing how that had generated wealth for the community, suggested that they buy a business.

He didn't want a going concern, but something he could build up for himself. All he had to do was find a suitable business then throw into it his energy, determination and motivation. As always, there was the double drive of wanting to do the best for his family and of showing his father he could succeed without him.

Early in 1996 Phil happened to see a signage business for sale for $10,000. It was the price rather than the type of business that caught his attention because he considered it shouldn't be too difficult to persuade a bank to lend such a modest sum. The prospect energised him. This was it, the business he would build up and make his own. Sure, there were a few problems to solve: he had no capital, knew nothing about the industry, and had no premises. On the plus side, he had energy, drive, and belief in his own abilities. Bev supported his ambitions, helping wherever she could.

He approached a bank for a loan, asking for the full $10,000. They turned him down. A father of seven young children, who had no equity and no permanent job, didn't add up to a good risk. He went to another bank, and another, until every bank in town had turned him down. As a last resort, Bev suggested he approach a building society. If they rejected his application he'd have to think of something else, but time was running out as the owner of the business wanted the deal settled.

Phil walked into the interview room, going over his pitch in his head. The woman behind the desk stood up to shake his hand. 'You're the dad with the six kids who rescued them from that cult, aren't you?'

That was the breakthrough. She'd been impressed by the magazine stories she'd read about him and wanted to give him a chance, apologising that the rules would only allow the society to lend him $6,000. But Phil was ecstatic. He was on the way. He borrowed $2,000 from a friend then put the offer to the vendor that he would pay $8,000 up front. If he couldn't pay the final $2,000 at the end of the first month, he would forfeit the lot. The vendor accepted the deal and the business was Phil's. It came with an old computer that he didn't even know how to turn on, and two days' training.

He involved the whole family in the first, hectic set-up months. They helped him deliver business cards all around town and were delighted when the first commission came in. It was to make a 'Happy Birthday' banner for Hungry Jack, the burger chain of the buy-one-get-one-free vouchers. Phil cut out the letters using the machine that came with the business, then got the children to help him lay it out. His building experience had given him layout skills but all the rest was trial and error.

Bev and the children helped wherever they could, touting for business by going through the Yellow Pages of the phone book and sending faxes to companies asking for their business. In the weekends and after school Israel would help his dad on the computer while the girls cleaned down any vehicles to be sign-written. Phil taught all of them how to apply the letters and they'd work together to squeegee them on then pull off the application tape. By the end of the month he was able to pay the vendor the remaining $2,000.

They were good months for the children, with their father around more of the time. They had a mother again. Their dad was happy, and suddenly there was more money. He gave them surprises and bought them presents. It was like Christmas happening every week. The whole process fascinated Israel. So this was what a business could do. It was a powerful thing if it could drag their family out of poverty. He began to wonder about a career involving business, though the idea of producing movies still attracted him. But then, neither might come to pass because he stayed home from school too often to do well.

The business took off. Phil loved the excitement of it, the buzz of the energy he could generate. He took on employees, read up on anything to do with signage that he could find, and expanded the business. Because of his ignorance when he started, he didn't know what could and couldn't be done. People would ask, 'Can you do this?' He would say yes, then later figure out how. His approach led to innovative ways of doing things and he learnt from the inevitable mistakes.

In May 1996 Neville's appeal against his sentence was heard in the Court of Appeal in Wellington. Only the most serious of the charges were prosecuted. Phil travelled to Wellington to hear the verdict. The sentence was upheld and Neville Cooper aka Hopeful Christian was sent to prison for five years on three charges of sexual assault.

The verdict was devastating for the community, with many almost losing their faith as a result. The hierarchy were secretive about the facts of the case, telling the community members that their leader was in prison because he was a Christian, just like Paul and Silas in the Bible who got imprisoned then went out and preached again. All the young ones believed it, and some of the older ones did, too.

Phil was relieved to return to Australia and immerse himself again in work.

Despite all the buzz and excitement of his burgeoning business, he never forgot that his actions had deprived his kids of their mother and he didn't want them to forget her. Neville had scuppered the attempts to keep in touch by letter, but it might be worth trying again to renew the contact now that his father was in prison.

He managed to track down Sandy's phone number, hoping that with Neville out of the way for the time being, Sandy would be free to be a mother even if only by phone. The children were excited; they were going to talk to their mum for the first time in four years. Crystal and Andreas were curious about her; Crystal had vague memories but to Andreas she was a complete stranger. The older four just wanted to hear her voice. Did she still remember them? Did she still love them? They weren't sure what to say to her, though. What would they talk about?

Israel put the call through with the phone on the speaker function so that they could all hear their mother talk. When Sandy answered, Israel managed to stammer out, 'Mum, it's Israel,' but was too emotional to say any more. The second that Dawn, Justine and Tendy heard her voice they burst into tears. Mum was there, talking to them. This was her voice. Memories flooded back.

Sandy was terrified. Why were they crying? Something awful must have happened. What was wrong?

Eventually she managed to calm them down enough to talk to them. There was nothing wrong? They were crying because they were so happy to talk to her? Well, whose fault was it that she couldn't be with them all the time? Their father's, that's whose fault it was. She switched from being motherly to preaching a diatribe cataloguing their father's sins.

The children cowered from the torrent of words. Israel and Dawn were old enough to have some understanding of why she was lecturing them about the terrible things their father had done, but it made no sense to the younger ones. They loved their dad and they knew he loved them, but they could detect no love in the way their mother spoke to them. None of them contacted her again for a long time.

Sandy's behaviour, Phil feels, shows how strongly she believed the community version of Neville's imprisonment. Phil was the villain who had made a martyr of his own father.

Neville served 18 months and was released early for good behaviour. He was reported as being a model prisoner who kept to himself and caused no problems. When he returned to Gloriavale he stepped down from his position as leader, saying that 'the bishop must be without blame'. Sandy's mother Naomi who was still in the community at the time said that after a few weeks God spoke to him and he stepped up again.

The community's pamphlet for visitors (*Life in Common: the experience of the Gloriavale Christian Community*) provides an insight into its daily life, in which Neville rejoices, and which for Phil proved impossible. As at Springbank, its ideal is of life according to Christian principles in a true Christian society where members love one another and put aside their own wills, independence and selfishness. Supporting biblical quotes are given: 'If any man will come after me, let him deny himself, and take up his cross, and follow me' (*Matthew 16:24*); 'He that believeth and is baptised shall be saved' (*Mark 16:16*).

Community living, the pamphlet explains, is the ideal way of organising, caring and providing for their large families, where 'it is hard to live a worldly, selfish life, but easy to find God's will and live in daily service to God.'

The Garden of Eden story is cited as evidence that God gave leadership to the man, and accordingly in Gloriavale women may not preach or expound on a biblical text; they may only read from the Bible. Despite this, all are considered equal, with leaders not privileged or exalted above others. (However, ex-members speak of a type of caste system where Coopers receive perks and privileges unavailable to non-Coopers.) Decisions on important matters are said to be made by the consensus of all, but whether that includes women is not stated.

Formal religious meetings are held on Sunday – or First Day. Everyone attends the First Day service to sing, listen to scripture, hear testimonies and break bread. Baptisms are conducted at these meetings, and foot-washing or prayers for the sick. Religion is part of daily life and informs everything a person does. Pagan references are abhorrent, thus the Easter bunny, Father Christmas, wedding rings and the tooth fairy are not welcome at Gloriavale. And as previously mentioned Christmas isn't celebrated and neither are birthdays.

Meals are shared in the dining hall where Neville/Hopeful often takes the opportunity to preach or rail against the outside world. Dress is modest and without adornment. Sexual purity is mandatory outside marriage. 'We do not tolerate homosexuality, fornication, adultery or remarriage of "divorced" people.' Divorce itself is not tolerated.

In the absence of contraception, many children are born, and are given names to inspire them. Although the pamphlet doesn't say so, Neville's is the final word on suitability. Appropriate names include Charity Love, Victory Overcomer and Willing Disciple.

The community borrows no money – an extremely challenging policy for Phil when he was running the business that kept the Springbank community financially viable in the late 80s.

Today, Gloriavale with its multi-million-dollar turnover, is economically important to the West Coast. The community spends locally, and takes no government benefits such as old age pensions. Their industries are run entirely with their own, unpaid labour: the pedigree Jersey herd has over 1200 cows; around 1400 deer provide venison, velvet and trophy heads; deer offal is rendered down and sold in powdered form. Gloriavale's men have always been innovative and have recently developed their own machinery to process sphagnum moss collected from the swamps of Glen Hopeful. These excellent mechanics run the only helicopter and aircraft maintenance business on the Coast. The extensive agricultural, building and mechanical activities provide employment and training for the young men.

Women's roles are much more limited. Their time is organised to let them meet their work commitments alongside family responsibilities. The baby centre, toddler centre, then play school, allow 'our mothers to contribute to the housework while their children are cared for' until they're old enough to start school. Unmarried women, 'single sisters', do more than their share of the women's work, knowing that once they are married, they will have the same assistance. However, it is reported that there are more young women in Gloriavale than there are young men to marry them and so a number won't be able to fulfil their calling, which is to marry and bear children. The recently established outreach community in India may provide a solution to the problem although that is not its stated aim.

Family is all-important: children are welcomed, and old people cared for, although some absconders say that no allowance is made for age and infirmity. Everyone is required to work as hard as they always have. Babies are born at home with the community midwife in attendance, although if there are problems the mother is hospitalised.

The section in the pamphlet entitled 'The Ladies' Realm', details the women's work. They cook around 7,000 meals and launder some 8,000 items weekly; the sewing women make all the clothes including underwear and concert costumes. Some supervise preschool and a few work in the office, and as telemarketers to overseas customers of the sphagnum moss industry. All this when they are also required to bear child after child, and do any seasonal work such as bottling fruit, or cutting up a butchered carcase for the freezer.

The community runs its own school which is inspected regularly by the Education Review Office whose reports are consistently good. Children go to school in the morning and work in the afternoon, doing community tasks. When a skill is needed that the community doesn't possess, a young person will go on to tertiary education, usually by distance learning.

Relaxation takes the form of picnics, music, and parties to celebrate weddings and other special events. Families also get several days of holiday each year when they may stay in the holiday house on the Glen Hopeful property, or take a community van elsewhere on the Coast.

As leader of his own utopia, Neville/Hopeful is a law unto himself, as his marriages also show. He said initially that if the leader's wife died, then the leader must remain celibate for the rest of his life. However, not long after Gloria's death, he married again, to a woman of 80. When she died he chose a new wife. She was 17 and he 50 years her senior. He now has a second family by her.

Towards the end of 1996, Neville's community was to receive one of his granddaughters back into the fold.

Gloria Cooper, Neville's first wife, with their six oldest children, c. 1962. Left to right: Hope, Charity (holding toys), Faith, Gloria holding John, Grace, Mercy.

Below: a still from a home movie of Neville and Gloria's family at an Australian beach, mid 1960s.

Above: a still from a home movie showing 'Voice of Deliverance' preacher and flock, Australia, 1960s.

Below: a still from a home movie of the 'Voice of Deliverance' tent, Australia, 1960s.

Above, left to right: Mark, Charity, Phil, Hope, Neville holding Miracle, Faith, Gloria holding Michael, Grace, Stephen, Mercy, John – Fielding, New Zealand, 1967.

Below: baptism in the duck pond built by Phil and Mark at Springbank, c. 1980.

Above: Sandy just before her marriage to Phil in 1981.

Below: girls from Springbank community knitting at a market day in Rangiora, c. 1985. On the left is Patience, the youngest Cooper daughter. *The Press*

Above: Neville at Springbank with the first accommodation block (Phil later abducted his children from this building) and the foundations of the second, 1983. *The Press*

Below: the back of the first accommodation block. Phil and his brother Mark are on the roof.

Above: Sandy and Phil on their wedding day shortly after Phil's nineteenth birthday, May 1981.

Right: Sandy at Springbank, c. 1985. She was pregnant with Justine.

Phil holding one-day-old Israel. (Phil had been building a pool table for the community four days earlier when he cut off his thumb with a Skilsaw. His thumb was reattached and a steel rod inserted.)

Above: school buildings at Springbank, Canterbury.

Below: Sandy in the kitchen at Springbank before the accommodation blocks and kitchen were built, c. 1988.

Above: Gloriavale buildings as seen in 'Children of the Mist' documentary. *60 Minutes/TV3*

Below: a still from undercover film footage of a concert given at Gloriavale. Sandy/Prayer is fourth from the right. *Melanie Reid/TV3*

Sandy holding Andreas, with Dawn (plaits) and Tendy while in the US.

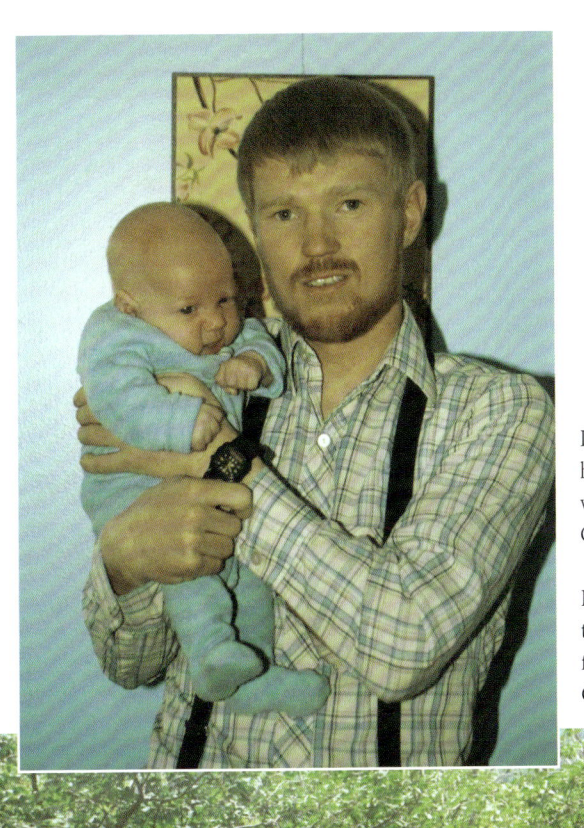

Left: Phil in Hutterite clothing, holding Andreas, February 1991, while living in the Woodcrest Community in New York state.

Below: Phil and children with their Hutterite surrogate family from the Catskills Mountains Community, 1992, after Sandy left.

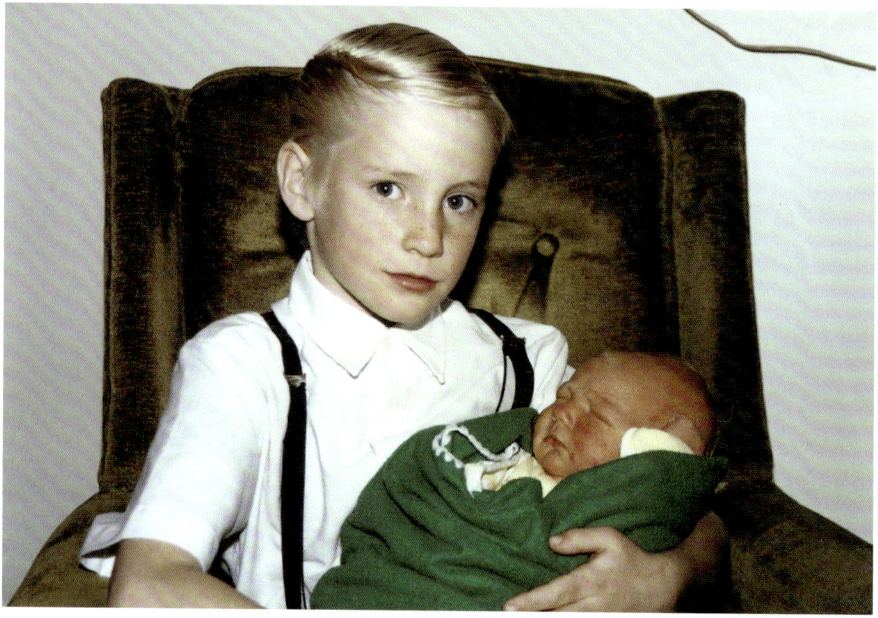

Above: Israel holding his six-day-old brother, Woodcrest Community, February 1991.

Left: Andreas in the Catskills Mountains Community riding the bike Phil made for Israel from wheelchair wheels and motor.

God Please Bring Our dear Mother Back to Us.

Why Mom is the Best

My Mom is the Best because she is loving and kind. She makes the best meals and she loves us kids. So much and I love her lots. I could give her a lot of kisses. She is the best mother in the world!

Above: the photo of Sandy that Phil kept on the table in each house the family moved to.

Left: the card that Dawn made soon after Sandy's departure, 1991.

Clockwise: Phil, Dawn, Israel, Tendy, Justine, Crystal, Andreas shortly after the family arrived in Australia in 1993. Dawn gave her mother this photo when she and her dad visited the community immediately after Phil found out about Cherish.

Above: 1993, in the first of the many houses Phil rented in and around Coffs Harbour in Australia. Clockwise: Phil, Crystal, Justine, Tendy, Dawn, Israel, Andreas. Sandy's photo is behind the milk bottle.

Below, left to right: Andreas, Justine, Crystal, Tendy, Mitchell, Israel, Bev, Phil in Coffs Harbour, 1997, taken a few months after Dawn's departure.

Above: a still from film footage of Gloriavale Christian Community, Lake Haupiri, 2006.
60 Minutes/TV3

Below, far back: Andreas, Phil; left to right: Israel's wife Jessica, Israel holding Zion, Mitch, Bev, Tendy, Crystal, Justine holding Annabelle, her husband Dion, Jess in front – Gold Coast, Australia, 2008.

CHAPTER THIRTEEN: DARK DAYS

It was awful, but I thought, okay Dawnie –
you're going back to see Mum. ISRAEL

Bev's life had been quiet and ordered before she moved in with Phil and into the maelstrom of his life. There was more to come, and what followed was hell for her, and for Phil the hardest period of his life.

Dawn's behaviour worsened as she entered adolescence. The dynamic between her, Israel, Justine and Tendy was changing as they all grew older. Partly this was due to Phil's increasing absences as the business absorbed his time, and partly it was normal teenage rebellion. While Crystal and Andreas still looked on Israel as their parent, Dawn, Justine and Tendy began to challenge his authority. Israel was 14, Dawn 13, Justine 11 and Tendy 10 when the girls began to gang up on him. They would tell him he wasn't the dad and they didn't have to do what he said. He retaliated by chasing them and when he caught them, would throw them into the swimming pool and make them cry. Life since their arrival in Australia three years before had never been smooth, but now it was increasingly chaotic, exacerbated by Phil's time and energies being consumed by his business.

One day Phil was horrified to discover the three girls in the bathroom, playing with matches, to the extent that the house was in danger of burning down. He was angry and the ensuing row sent Dawn fleeing to the sanctuary of Carol and Nina's house where she ranted against her father. The upshot was that she accused him of molesting her.

Officers from the Department of Community Services called Phil in for an interview. He had nothing to hide and naïvely believed that if he told the truth then all would be well. In answer to their question about whether anything inappropriate had ever happened between him and his daughter he told them of a night soon after they had arrived in Australia. Dawn had climbed into his bed for comfort, as all the kids did more often than not. He woke abruptly from a deep sleep to find that he had his hand on her. He got such a fright he leapt straight out of bed and stood there shaking. Thoughts of his father's behaviour raced through his head and he was so upset that he might be following in Neville's footsteps, even unwittingly, that he rushed off to see a doctor in the morning. The doctor was reassuring. Phil had been dreaming, nothing had been intentional and no, he definitely shouldn't talk to Dawn about it. She hadn't woken and he hadn't actually done anything to her. The doctor advised that, as a single man, it would be best not to have the children in his bed, but he acknowledged their need for comfort and therefore, on balance, it would do more harm than good to ban them from their father's bed.

Even though Phil showed the Community Services officers the doctor's report, the story was enough to condemn him in the eyes of the Department.The officers interviewed the other children at school, bewildering them. Why were these people asking such strange questions? Why did they want to know if their father ever touched them? Tendy told them that her dad would give her a whack on the backside sometimes, and a woman took her away to see if the marks were still there. But they all said no, their dad never did anything bad to them and they couldn't understand what the whole drama was about. When they got home, Phil took them to the beach where he tried to explain that Dawn was going to be living with a foster family, and why. They were upset to see their father crying and couldn't grasp what he was trying to tell them about their sister.

Carol and Nina offered to foster Dawn but they were deemed unsuitable foster parents due to the fact that they both said they'd been sexually abused as children. Dawn was sent to strangers, and after a day or two, she rang up saying she wanted to come home, but Bev had to tell her she wasn't allowed. Dawn, who had so sorely missed her mother, was now adrift without any family at all.

The family later found out that Carol and Nina had played on Dawn's desperation to have a mother and had coached her in what to say in an accusation against Phil, telling her it would mean she could come and live with them. The other children now suspect that the Department of Community Services knew Phil was innocent but they had to be seen to be doing the right thing. Their solution to the problem was to give Dawn the choice of going to live in foster care, or of returning to her own mother. As far as Dawn was concerned, the choice was easy. She knew little of the reality of the community whereas she loved her mother fiercely. Her accusations had cut her off from the other mother-figures in her life and she craved a motherly presence. She chose her own mother – who was living under the aegis of a convicted paedophile, an aspect of the situation that was ignored by the authorities. It worried Israel and Phil deeply that they didn't take that into consideration. They knew what had happened in the community and should know that abuse might still be going on.

Phil did his best to prevent Dawn having to return to the community. He gave the Department of Community Services copies of the documentaries, telling them that this was what she would be going back to. 'I will never see her again, and you are signing her death warrant.'

They replied that she was going back to her mother. Phil had the option, they said, of going through the courts to gain custody, but in any case they would make sure somebody in New Zealand monitored the situation and send him reports. That didn't happen.

He considered taking it to court, but the odds were so heavily stacked against him that he knew it would be useless to try. He had no money, whereas the community by now was wealthy. He'd not long met Bev and was trying to keep everything together and balanced, but the other children were being pulled apart by what was happening. He felt more vulnerable than he ever had, so in the end decided to let this one child go for the sake of the others.

It was a decision that cost him dearly because, ever since, the guilt of it has weighed on him. Should he have fought harder? Could he have?

When the children learned that Dawn was going back to their mother, they didn't realise it would be forever, and they suspect she didn't know it, either. As part of the community, she wouldn't be allowed to have a relationship with her Australian family, and Phil was aware that he would probably never see her again. He pretended optimism in front of the others, telling them not to worry because Dawn would come back and they'd all be together again. One part of him was happy, excited even, that Dawn was going to be with her mother, and he hired a private movie company in New Zealand to film their reunion at Christchurch Airport. The movie would be just for the family, a reminder of Dawn and reassurance for them all that she was happy to be back with her mum. They bought her comics and puzzle books for the plane trip and went to the airport to see her off. Tendy envied Dawn and for a long time afterwards, whenever she was in trouble, would say that she wanted to go and live with her mum, but she and the younger ones had no understanding of what that would mean.

Carol and Nina hadn't got what they wanted, but Israel was bitter that their actions had further fractured his family. He would hear his father crying at night for weeks afterwards. Dawn's accusations made Phil revisit the question of whether he'd done the right thing in taking the children away from their mother, even though it had meant rescuing them from Neville. Israel remembers him saying that Neville was right after all; he, Phil, was cursed because God was taking his children away from him.

He had done his best to fight the bureaucracy so that he could keep his family intact, but he had lost. Dawn had gone and he had to accept it.

The whole episode nearly broke Phil. The question dogged him all through their growing up: would the children be better off if they'd stayed with their mother in the community?

After she'd been back in the community for a couple of years, Dawn wrote to Phil, apologising for lying. Nina too later apologised to Phil for her part in the deception. She even went so far as to travel to Gloriavale to try and persuade Dawn to leave.

Phil hasn't seen Dawn since the day she left and isn't allowed to contact her. It was six years before her siblings saw her again.

CHAPTER FOURTEEN:
CHAOS OF THE TEEN YEARS

Dad would try all these new rules, trying to organise us all.
We'd sit down and have this big family meeting at night.
I used to hate it and be dramatic about it – I just wanted
things the way they used to be. TENDY

Towards the middle of 1996, everyone rejoiced at the happy news that Bev was pregnant. Tendy felt special when Bev told her before she told the other kids.

In 1997 Phil's business was doing well enough for him to buy a property in the country where he built a shed to use as a base. He took on six employees, but with his usual generosity in helping others, he would give a job to the neediest person rather than to the best one.

The move to the country didn't help the family dynamics, and chaos sometimes reigned unchecked when the children were alone. Phil tried to impose order, with family meetings in the evenings to introduce schemes that involved lists of chores and rewards of stickers. Tendy who was 11 when they moved to the country hated it all. She looks back now and can laugh at memories of getting all dramatic at the meetings, when she would keep repeating, 'I just want it to be like it used to be.'

Phil wasn't around enough to enforce any new system. The children were on their own after school and for long periods in the holidays. They suffered their father's unreliability and accepted it as normal, knowing that they would be the last ones to be picked up from sports practices, or that any arrangements they made would be broken if something came up at work.

To Phil, being able to provide for his family was essential; it was what a good father did. It was important to him that he could buy things they needed, give them holidays, and surprise them with treats; it was how he showed them he loved them. He would shower them with expensive treats whenever he came back from long periods away. Interestingly, Neville had done the same thing when Phil was a child. He'd be away on his tent campaigns or speaking tours and come back laden with gifts for the children.

Although Phil was a loving and generous father, he wasn't able to see that what they needed most was his time and presence. They'd been through so much, but he couldn't help them overcome the issues arising out of their past because he hadn't dealt with them himself. He just kept going, staying positive for them and doing what he was good at, which was making money for them. His absenteeism made Bev's life just about impossible as she struggled with trying to be a stepmother to his strong willed bunch who were so used to having their own way.

Jessica was born in February 1997, another little blond-haired Cooper.

Bev had a new baby, her own son Mitchell who was not quite four years old, and Phil's five children to parent, often single-handedly.

Bev and Phil married once Phil's divorce from Sandy came through in October. Crystal was pleased. It felt like she had a real mother at last, although the wedding brought questions for the nine-year-old from her friends about where her real mother was. She opted for simplicity, saying her mum lived in New Zealand and they didn't see much of her. It was easier than saying she lived in a cult, then having to explain what a cult was.

By the end of 1997, the good relationship between Bev and Tendy foundered as Tendy and Justine became more and more rebellious. Justine was 12, a year older then Tendy, and where she led, Tendy followed. They were either the best of friends or fighting to the death, with Bev having to cope with the fallout. Justine was headstrong and now she was doing exactly as she pleased. She'd bring cigarettes home for her and Tendy to smoke. Phil tried to stop them by using the psychological approach. He bought a packet of cigarettes, sat the girls down, and lectured them on the evils of tobacco use. When he figured the message had hit home he left the room, leaving the smokes behind as an awful warning. The lecture had no effect and the girls grabbed the cigarettes, thrilled with their windfall of free smokes.

Israel's difficulties weren't behavioural but were just as serious. His academic achievement by the end of his second year of high school was abysmal. Phil, already guilty about him missing out on his childhood, didn't want him to grow up without an education as well, and suggested that he go to boarding school. It also meant he'd be out from under Bev's feet at home.

Israel agreed to go, although he hated leaving the children he regarded as his own. They'd been such a close family it was hard for him to settle in a new situation but school was another community and turned out to be a bit like living with a whole lot of brothers. It was a Catholic school with strange rituals and, weirdly for him, he saw similarities between the community and the Catholicism Neville abhorred.

Boarding school felt initially like the worst thing that had ever happened to Israel, but turned out to be one of the best. He caught up on the schooling he'd lost and excelled academically, but perhaps more importantly for a 15-year-old, it helped him to accept his history and to feel more a part of the world he now lived in. When he first arrived, he repeated his fictional stories about his family, but his classmates picked up on discrepancies and kept questioning him until he told the truth. It was a relief to stop hiding.

For the whole of his first year, he kept pretty much to himself, immersing himself in study because there was nothing else to do. He was used to getting up early at home and continued to do so at school, using the two or three hours before breakfast to study. During this year he taught himself how to study by reading everything he could: text books that weren't part of the class requirement; re-reading work done during class; reading around each subject in every reference he could find. His grades improved as he filled in the gaps in his previous schooling.

It wasn't until the second year that he began to make friends and, as he did, he reduced the intensity of his study regime, although he still maintained a rigorous schedule to ensure he didn't fall behind again. By his final year, the school and his peers had come to recognise his capacity for taking on responsibility, making him a prefect and a house sports captain. Israel relished the responsibilities which included the care and welfare of the younger boys. He was happy to return to the nurturing, caring roles that had so long been part of his life at home.

At home Phil's business continued to grow. It was the challenge he loved, the feeling of being in the midst of chaos and controlling six different things at once. It absorbed and fascinated him.

However it absorbed his time as well and Bev was left to deal with Justine and Tendy who were increasingly out of control, getting into trouble and always fighting. On the home front, the family struggled with issues that Phil could ignore as long as he buried himself in work.

At Christmas 1998 Phil took all of them to New Zealand for the holidays. It was good for them to be with the wider family again and the whole clan attended church on Christmas Day.

One day they decided on the spur of the moment to go to the West Coast and visit their mother and sisters in the community. Phil drove the children over but he knew they wouldn't be let in if the community saw he was with them, so he and Jess got out of the van at the gate while Bev drove the others into the grounds. They were driving around looking for the right building when they caught a glimpse of Dawn among a group of people. She looked shocked to see them, like a deer in the headlights, and vanished when the group scattered at the sight of a strange vehicle. Later Israel realised she would have been indoctrinated in the belief that outsiders were evil and that her own siblings weren't good Christians. She would also have been swept up by the group around her whose instinct was to run when an unknown vehicle approached. The community was very sensitive to the possibility of further abductions.

Bev started the engine again and they finally found where they were meant to go. The moment they pulled up, Neville/Hopeful and his second-in-command came out of the building and strode over to the van where Hopeful demanded to know why they were there. Bev told him she'd brought the children to see their mother. He asked who Bev was. Phil's wife? He already had a wife thus Bev was an adulteress, a whore. He fired an entire repertoire of abusive names at her while the younger children cowered, crying, in the back of the van. Bev didn't want to leave until they had seen their mother, but Israel knew it was never going to happen and told her to just go. The younger ones cried most of the way back to Christchurch. The visit strengthened Israel's belief that his dad had been right to take them out of the community. It gave Justine, Tendy and Crystal first-hand insight into his reasons for doing so, but for seven-year-old Andreas it was simply upsetting.

CHAPTER FIFTEEN: CHANGING DIRECTION

Justine went to school with our kids. She had lots of issues but lots of talent too. She was struggling with the whole rejection thing, but she buried it. FAITH

When they returned to Australia, Phil and Bev decided it would be good for them all to start attending church as a family. Bev hadn't grown up in a religious family although she did attend a Catholic school. She liked the idea of being part of a church community and together she and Phil sought out one that suited them both, hoping that shared worship would bring them closer and lead to positive changes in Justine and Tendy's behaviour. Israel, Crystal and Andreas accepted the regime change. To Israel it felt like a connection to happier times in his life, first in the New Zealand community when he was very young, then later with the Hutterites. Justine and Tendy were unimpressed. Tendy hated what she saw as hypocrisy. There they were, pretending to be the perfect family sitting together in church, when their reality was more like chaos and mayhem. She refused to play the game of happy families. No way was she going to pretend to be a good Christian girl. Instead, she perfected the role of offended drama queen.

Justine and Tendy, increasingly stroppy and strong-willed, ignored all rules. They got into trouble and they didn't care. Bev was often by herself, trying to discipline them when Phil was out of the country on business or buried in work at the office. By 2001, desperately worried that they were on the point of wrecking their lives, Phil phoned Faith to ask her if she'd take one of them. She discussed it with her family and they decided to take Justine because, like them, she was keen on sport. However Tendy had thought she would be the one to go, and when she discovered it was Justine, she was angry, blaming Justine for manipulating the situation in her favour. Justine had mixed feelings about leaving home. Living in a new country would be exciting, but she wasn't sure whether life with Faith would be so good.

Faith was under no illusions about how difficult it would be to take her niece under her wing. She feels now that she was too strict with her, something Justine heartily agrees with, although she also credits Faith with saving her from making a huge mess of her life. She stayed with Faith for three years until she was 18 and finished school. Once she settled in, she loved school because it was big on sport and she made lasting friendships. Her new friends didn't smoke and didn't think it was cool so she quit the cigarettes along with the other anti-social behaviour. While she was living with Faith, Justine began to appreciate the value of the religious beliefs the family lived by and she herself became a Christian.

With her partner-in-crime living in another country, 14-year-old Tendy was finding life hard. Justine was in a good school, whereas Tendy was still changing schools often and still with her bad group of friends. She hated going to church, and the way she saw her family pretending they were all happy and wonderful whenever anyone was around. She wouldn't play the game and refused to smile when she had to be in a family photo. She felt that all the others could pretend, but she couldn't. She was the emotional one, the one who wore her heart on her sleeve. Her behaviour worsened: she climbed out the window at night; she wandered around town until a desperate Phil finally found her; she smoked and drank. At home, she spun every incident into a drama designed to prove how much her family hated her. One night she climbed out the window to go joy-riding with boys. When she came back, Bev was waiting for her at the end of the drive, worried sick. They had a huge row but Tendy was unrepentant. She ran to her bedroom and phoned her father who was in Thailand on business. 'Help! She's psycho! She's going to kill me!' She spun it so that Bev was an evil witch-woman and she the hapless victim. It worked. Phil flew home immediately.

Whereas Tendy was more and more alienated from the church, it became increasingly important for the rest of the family. Bev got involved in various church-run activities and one day attended a lecture given by a woman working in an orphanage the church supported in a remote area of Borneo in Indonesia. She came home enthusing about the amazing work being done there. Phil astonished her by telling her she should go and visit the place to see it for herself.

Balai Karangi village in the province of Kalamatan was not a tourist destination. Getting there would require three separate flights into areas increasingly remote from the English-speaking world, but the orphanage had captured Bev's heart and she decided to go. Phil suggested she take Tendy with her for company but also in the hope that the trip would shock her into seeing that her own life was paradise compared with how others had to live.

The trip in September 2001 went well. Tendy loved having

Bev all to herself and the two of them got on well, the way they had when Bev first arrived in the family. Balai Karangi village welcomed them. Tendy with her blond hair was an exotic novelty and streams of children flocked around her wherever she went. They tugged her hand, pulling her with them to show her the hospital the church was building, and the orphanage. The people of the village had nothing but the ragged clothes they wore and their diet consisted of rice three times a day, yet they were so happy just to be alive.

When they got home to Australia, Tendy went right back to being what she now describes as a little shit, but the visit had been transformative for Bev. She wanted them all to go over and experience for themselves the happiness of people who had nothing and who lived without any modern-world essentials. Phil jumped at the idea. Here was a project he could make happen, one that would help bring his family together. He threw his energy into raising the money to pay for airfares for all eight family members. They would go as soon as possible.

His business couldn't afford all the airfares so he swung into a round of fund-raising. Brunei Airlines agreed to sponsor some of the flights. Business friends he approached donated money for the trip and to buy materials for the building projects at the orphanage and hospital complex.

Although the trip did no more for the children than paper over the cracks of their family life, it did leave a lasting impression on all of them, by putting their own history into some perspective. They felt they had life pretty good in comparison with the villagers, especially the orphans.

Phil worked on the building projects, glad to use his expertise for such a worthwhile cause. Bev helped out in the orphanage and the kids roamed the village surrounded by a crowd of local children who attached themselves like magnets whenever Bev's son Mitchell or one of the Cooper kids appeared outside.

The visit did bring the family closer. The kids loved having their dad around in this haven from the outside world. His business back home couldn't intrude because there was no internet and no phone coverage either. They were in the middle of a jungle high in the mountains in 30 degree heat, where they were pummelled by rain and thunder storms every day, and they loved it.

Phil saw what a difference his and Bev's little help had made. When he got home again he launched into a round of fund-raising, starting with a charity ball which raised thousands of dollars for the Mount Hope project in Balai Karangi village. It was a huge undertaking but he loved it; it was like the best days in the community when he masterminded the concerts.

He and Bev have been back several times and they continue to support the orphanage and hospital with money and labour. In 2006 Phil opened a letter which contained a cheque for $15,000. It was from the recently established Hutterite community in Australia who had heard of his work at Mount Hope. He read to Bev the message that came with it: 'God has blessed us and we know that you will use this to bless others.'

They immediately put it toward the support of the orphanage.

All the family were elated by their experience at the orphanage, but once back home again, cracks reappeared in the family structure.

CHAPTER SIXTEEN:
ESCAPE FROM GLORIAVALE

Some of the adults who come in get converted to the community but not to Christianity and they can still be rotten old sinners. NAOMI

Not many people leave Gloriavale now, partly because of its isolation, but also because the young ones have grown up inside and know no other way of life.

Phil's family offered hospitality to one young man who had left because he wanted to work with computers, but inside the community one does not choose and he was apprenticed to a painter. He hated it and decided to leave. To avoid being caught and hauled in front of the men, he walked across the swamp at the back of the farm and hitchhiked to Christchurch. The whole operation took him 14 hours.

Naomi's escape was different. The children's maternal grand-mother had been growing more and more disillusioned with Neville who once referred to himself as the angel of Gloriavale. She whispered to her son that if that was the case, his halo had slipped. Her son shushed her for fear somebody would hear and report her.

Naomi was in charge of the shopping which gave her the freedom to go into town once a week to buy groceries. On one such trip, while the community was still at Springbank, she was put in touch with her friend who had left years before. The friend showed her a video, warning her not to shut her mind against it because it was the truth. Naomi was devastated to see her own daughter, Sandy's sister Yvette who had left the community, describing in harrowing detail the way in which Neville had sexually violated her.

A few years later at Gloriavale, Naomi felt increasingly that Neville was no longer preaching the word of God and she knew she couldn't be wholehearted in her commitment. She felt that true religion was being squeezed out of Gloriavale and that she was dying inside spiritually. It took her two years to make the decision to leave because it was such a hard thing to do. She had family there, grandchildren and great-grandchildren, and she loved her job, helping in the school where she was confidante to the children who all called her Grandma. On the other hand, she was constantly in pain from chronic arthritis and physically couldn't handle the work. Neville told her she was getting lazy and that she didn't have the spirit, that she was just giving in. In *What We Believe* he writes, 'Christians should learn to bear pain and hardship as part of the corruption of this life'. He told her off and when she broke down, he said, 'Don't you cry!'

She retorted, 'I'll cry if I want to,' but then thought, oh, now I'm in trouble.

Neville knew she didn't like him.

She planned her escape carefully. The first step was to get money but she was only 64 so not entitled to the old-age pension. However, Work and Income in Greymouth arranged a benefit for her of $146 a week which she had credited directly into her newly opened bank account. She asked the bank not to send her any mail, and waited several weeks for the money to accumulate. She left in April 2002, without telling anybody because if she had they would have tried to talk her out of it or, worse, she would have been called to front up to the men who would wear her down until she agreed to stay.

She drove the shopping vehicle into Greymouth earlier than usual, telling people that she had a hospital appointment, a lie which troubled her conscience for some time. She prayed all the way into town, *Please God, don't let this truck break down.*

She caught the bus to Nelson and when it stopped at Pancake Rocks she rang the community and told them to pick up the vehicle from the Mitre 10 car park. They thought she must have been admitted to hospital, but she just said, 'No, I'm not coming back,' and hung up.

Naomi felt dreadful about leaving, and full of guilt. She prayed for forgiveness for leaving and for telling the lie. But she knew that everyone felt guilty when they left and that she'd been right to do it. In Nelson she rented a basic cabin in a motor camp and clothed herself from second-hand shops. She sent the blue dress back. It was almost new and somebody would be able to use it.

Unlike Faith, she didn't suffer from the fear she would be damned to hell for leaving and instead she felt she'd got her religion back again. Now she was able to worship God the way she'd done before Neville clamped the iron control on the community. She was able to return to the tenets she believed to be right. The relief was huge, of not having to look over her shoulder for Neville or one of the men whenever she did something as simple as trim her hair and put it in curlers. The thing that tore at her heart was leaving her family behind: a son, another daughter, and both their families, as well as Sandy and Dawn. She knew it was unlikely she'd ever see them again and she'd been too frightened of discovery to seek out Phil's family or Yvette.

Before long, the family heard the news, which cheered them immensely: Naomi had escaped from Gloriavale and gone into hiding. Nobody knew where she was, but Phil hired a private detective who discovered she was living in a caravan at Tahuna Beach Motor Camp in Nelson. Israel rang her up, but instead of being delighted to hear from him, she was terrified. 'How did you get this number? Who told you I was here? How did you find out where I am? I don't want you ringing here.' She refused to talk and hung up.

Her reaction stunned them. They'd been looking forward to a joyous reunion with their much-loved grandma and couldn't believe she didn't want anything to do with them. But Phil, true to form, refused to give up. He knew Naomi would be suffering because of leaving her family, and from lack of money. He enlisted the help of Naomi's long-time friend who had left the community years earlier, asking her to persuade Naomi to let Israel talk to her. Eventually she agreed and he was able to persuade her to accept Phil's typically generous offer of tickets for Australia. She lived with the family for several months and the reunion was everything the children had hoped for. Crystal and Andreas had no memories of her, but the others all recognised her and remembered her playing with them, teasing them and singing with them. Her grandmother was balm to Tendy. She never felt any criticism from her and Tendy felt that if ever she became a Christian herself, she'd be the same sort of Christian as her Grandma was.

Naomi was with Phil's family for Christmas 2002, as was the young man who had also escaped from the community. When

Naomi asked him what he'd like for Christmas, the other children told her to buy him fudge. She went into town, found a sweet shop, but then had to ring home to ask what flavour. They laughed and told her it was hair product he wanted, and that they were teaching him how to live in the world. Naomi couldn't believe anyone, especially a young man, would spend a whole $16 on stuff to go on his hair.

She stayed with the family for several months before she went to help nurse her dying sister in Brisbane. The children were thrilled to have their grandmother living with them. Israel had been worried that she would be different, but she was exactly the same loving, funny grandma he remembered from when he was little. Tendy adored her and saw her as the one who was a true Christian. She never preached at Tendy or told her off, always loving her no matter what she did.

And Tendy did plenty. Coming up to her sixteenth birthday that December, she put Bev and Phil through hell. Phil sat her down and tried to make her see sense. He was worried about her, and that her wild behaviour was affecting the younger ones. She decided to interpret this as meaning he wanted her to leave home, so she had her birthday and went.

She travelled up and down the coast, drifting from job to job, smoking and drinking and making one bad choice after another. She'd drift home again, move on soon afterwards, and go back into the same destructive lifestyle. Her life hit rock-bottom time and again. Phil tried to help her but her behaviour went against every value he believed in. She wasn't interested in his recently reclaimed Christianity and it further alienated her.

Tendy met a boy, moved in with him and got pregnant although she didn't discover that until they'd broken up. He didn't want anything to do with her and used threats to make her stay away from him, possibly because he'd now got the next girlfriend pregnant, too.

Tendy was in debt, she was drinking and smoking heavily, and pregnant. In the end, she got desperate and rang Israel in Brisbane where he was at university doing a business degree. She poured out her troubles to the brother who had always been the stable, reliable presence in her life. He and Justine clubbed together to bring her home, and persuaded her to tell Phil and Bev. That was good because now she had her family around her again, but bad because, as Christians, they didn't want her to have an abortion. Tendy didn't know what she wanted, but she knew that it was her life and she'd have to make a decision soon.

It was Christmas, and again Phil took them all to Christchurch. Before they left he suggested to Crystal that she ring the community to ask if they could visit their mother and Dawn while they were in New Zealand. Crystal wasn't keen after the previous experience, but in the end she rang; they were given permission, and pressed to stay for a few days. She declined the invitation to stay, saying that they'd just go for the day. The family flew to New Zealand and on the day of the appointment Bev drove them over to the coast. The children hadn't wanted her to come because they didn't want her abused the way she had been the time before, but Phil insisted, knowing they'd be tired and need her when they came back. They dressed carefully, keeping in mind the community's attitude to dress, however the girls didn't have any long skirts so they all opted for jeans that weren't tight, and loose jumpers. Crystal braided her hair. Justine had a nose-ring and for some reason she's now unable to fathom, didn't take it out.

The visit began well enough with their mother and Dawn

coming out to meet them. It was the first time they'd seen Dawn for about six years and they were excited to be with her again. Then Neville/Hopeful came out and invited them to come inside and sit down. Once he had them captive he got stuck into them: 'Why do you dress like men?' 'Our women dress modestly and it's beautiful.' 'Only pigs wear rings in their noses.' He kept turning to Sandy, demanding her agreement, calling her by her new name of Prayer.

Sandy/Prayer was distressed by her children's worldly appearance. But the floor was Hopeful's. He lectured them about how they had chosen to live with their evil father in a world of adultery and wickedness. Israel spoke up but Hopeful refuted everything with biblical quotes. Justine said something, too, but that was a major mistake: she was a woman and her place was to be quiet, meek and obedient. The older kids felt sorry for Andreas. He was only 11 and shouldn't have to suffer this tirade against his own father. Also, he was the only one who had no memory of their mother. Crystal could at least remember her face, and the older ones had definite memories, but Andreas just had to sit there listening to his grandfather while this stranger nodded in response to Hopeful saying, 'Isn't that so, Prayer?' 'You tell them, Prayer.' All of them noticed that she didn't directly agree that their father was all the terrible things Hopeful said he was.

They sat quiet and endured, waiting for it to be over. At last they were allowed to go with their mother and Dawn to their rooms, and the day improved. However, Hopeful hovered around, never leaving them alone for long with their mother. When he wasn't there, Sandy was more like herself and talked about when they were little. Dawn told them her memories of living in Australia.

The best thing was meeting ten-year-old Cherish. She looked

like Justine and Andreas, but they could all see traces of their own faces in hers. It was the highlight of the day, but she was only allowed to stay with them for a couple of minutes before she had to go and do her chores. Tendy suspects they were trying to protect her from evil influences, or perhaps from being seduced by her worldly siblings.

Whenever Hopeful was in the room, conversation faltered and they couldn't say what they wanted to. All the time, too, the meeting they'd been subjected to when they arrived hung over them, but they tried to simply enjoy being with Dawn and their mother. The day was charged with a whole mix of emotions and was extremely tiring. It ended with Hopeful and their mother driving them around the community, with Hopeful conducting the tour as if he were trying to sell the place. They felt like strangers, like people he'd never met before. Towards the end, he leaned towards Sandy and they held a whispered conversation.

Their mother turned around and told her children again how disappointed she was that they were so worldly and that in a way it might have been better had she not given birth to them. Her parting words were that unless they came to be with her in the community and live the way she did, then this would be the last time they met and that she'd never see them again.

Then Bev arrived with the van. Sandy demanded to know what *she* was doing there; the atmosphere cooled noticeably and they climbed in with Bev and drove away. The children each made their own interpretation of the incident.

Israel: 'I could understand on some level that it hadn't been my mother saying those hurtful things, that it was just the community rhetoric and that she'd been manipulated into saying them. But it doesn't make the pain any less, of hearing your mother say that.'

Justine: 'On the way home, Bev was asking us what happened, and then it pretty much hit us. The whole way home we were quiet – a bit of crying, too, and I kept thinking, oh my gosh, did that really happen? She doesn't want any contact with us from now on. Oh my gosh, we're never going to see her again. What a way to leave, to finish it.'

Tendy: 'We just left with no nice goodbye. We were all so upset and so exhausted. Just to go there and be ripped apart by your mother you hadn't seen for years, and to see your sister – and all the mixed emotions. It was so exhausting and I remember sleeping the whole way back. We were crying and then we all fell asleep. I remember Mum saying she was disappointed and how in a way it would have been better if she hadn't had us because of the way we were living and how we turned out. But I never took it that she wished she had never had us. I know that Justine and the rest of the kids did, but I never felt it was said like that.'

Crystal: 'Oh! Crush the day! We went away and we were all just silent on the way home. We all slept so we didn't have to cry. It was a bit hard having your mum talk like that, even if she hasn't been in our life that much.'

CHAPTER SEVENTEEN: FALLOUT

*I'd got to the end of myself and I didn't want to live this
day-to-day life where I had to worry about bills and stress.
So I had this idea: I'm just going to go and live in the community.
I'm just going to go. I don't care. I knew what it was like but
I didn't care.* TENDY

The visit with their mother affected all the children. For Justine it compounded the stress she felt coping with her school work, living away from home, and having to say goodbye to her family for another six months. She went through a bad patch of depression when she couldn't go on pretending she didn't care that her mother had left her. She spent a lot of time talking with Faith and was finally able to confront some of what she felt about her mother leaving them.

Israel, back at university in Brisbane, struggled to understand how God who was supposed to love his children had allowed their family to suffer so much hurt. He more or less abandoned his religion and became extremely cynical. He argued with his father about the way Phil had handled things in the past, and now that Israel was studying business he wasn't slow in telling him that he disagreed with his business methods, too. Relations between them were strained but they were managing to get along until Israel brought home his best friend from university. Phil recognised at once the manipulative control this young man exerted over his son, but Israel wouldn't hear any criticism of his friend, which quickly escalated the tensions between father and son.

One evening the whole situation blew up, ending with Phil giving Israel an ultimatum: Do what I want or you're not part of this family. It's my way or the highway.

At the time, he didn't even hear the echo of Neville.

Israel chose the highway, walked out of the house, and returned to Brisbane. He remained estranged from his father and his sense of isolation was extreme. Bubbling away underneath everything was the revelation that his mother was sorry she had given birth to him. That visit to her in Gloriavale affected the four older children deeply.

For Tendy, the visit was just one more addition to the mess her life was in. She was a disappointment to her mother, even though Sandy knew nothing about the pregnancy. Tendy still had no idea what she was going to do about the baby, but the decision was taken out of her hands when she had a miscarriage. Her life continued to spiral downwards. She was desperately unhappy, hurting emotionally, and directionless. Her finances were a mess and so were her personal relationships. She kept pushing people away and didn't care who she hurt in the process.

The community suddenly seemed like a haven, a place where her problems would be taken from her, where she wouldn't have to think or to worry. They would look after her and they would love her. She rang Sandy and told her she wanted to come over and live there. That call led to hours of phone conversation with her mother over about three weeks. When Sandy criticised Phil, Tendy let her. All her problems were her father's fault and she

187

refused to stick up for him. Under Sandy's influence, she became a Christian. She rang all the friends she'd hurt, asking them to forgive her.

Despite her new-found faith, she still felt desperate, but the community was starting to seem less of an attractive solution. She turned again to Israel and again poured out her troubles to him. His own life was a mess but one of 'his' children had asked for help and he gave it. He listened to her, then suggested that she pray about it and ask God to help her, failing to mention that he was questioning his own Christian commitment. She took his advice and also decided to tell Sandy she would go to stay in the community, but only for a couple of months. She wouldn't commit herself to saying she'd stay forever.

The community bought her air tickets, but they didn't want her to spend time with Justine in Christchurch beforehand. However, Tendy hadn't been schooled to obedience; she wanted to spend a week with her sister and they could like it or lump it. The prospect of her visit led to communication between the inside and outside members of the family. Justine was able to tell her mother and Dawn about her engagement when she rang to discuss arrangements for them to collect Tender-Joy from Justine's house.

When Tendy arrived, Justine showed her the nightgown Dawn had made her for her wedding night. It wasn't exactly the last word in sexy lingerie.

As the week went by Tendy got nervous about the whole idea of staying in the community. Maybe she'd go for just six weeks, or a month – perhaps two weeks. Sandy and Dawn came to pick her up from Justine's and were delighted to see her. Justine kept aloof, wary after the disastrous visit to the community, but she took the opportunity to invite them to her wedding. Sandy's response was to ask if Phil would be there. Justine said, 'Of course he will be.' She wasn't surprised when her mother said she wouldn't go anywhere within a thousand metres of where *he* was.

Justine didn't argue. There was no point. 'Come and stand at the back of the church if you'd like to.' Sandy didn't commit herself to that either and Justine was pretty sure neither of them would come, but she felt good that she'd been able to ask her and that she and Dawn had met Dion, her fiancé.

Tendy, Sandy and Dawn talked non-stop all the way back to Gloriavale. Tendy's spirits lifted. It had been a good decision to come. This was her mum and it was so great to see her sister again. When they arrived at Gloriavale, people crowded round to welcome her. Loving family surrounded her; she was royalty and nothing was too much trouble. Dawn and Sandy took her to their dormitory where they had prepared a top bunk for her, making it up with the silk-covered doona Dawn had sewn for her. Tendy climbed up and found the platter of nuts and chocolates they'd put there especially for her.

They gave her a blue dress to wear in place of the jeans and jumper she'd arrived in. Okay, she thought, I can do this.

She went into the bathroom to change, and burst out laughing at the girl in the mirror who looked like a total idiot in the long blue dress. When she came out, everyone told her how lovely she looked.

Hopeful sat down beside her. He put his hand on her leg and told her how beautiful she was. She wanted to yell at him to take his hand off her, but she didn't want to get kicked out. It took all her resolution not to react. This was the man who'd caused so much hurt in her life; she knew all the stories of what he'd done, and now here he was with his hand on her leg, telling her she was beautiful and how happy they all were that she was here.

Everywhere she went in the community, people came up to her and welcomed her. She met aunts, uncles, cousins, and everyone called her Tender-Joy. She met another girl called Tender-Joy whose parents had named her in honour of Sandy/Prayer's lost children. She discovered that her mother had enormous status in the community because she was the one who had been willing to give up her children for the love of God; she was the one who had made an immense sacrifice.

The best thing about the visit was getting to know ten-year-old Cherish. They clicked immediately so that Tendy found it hard to believe she hadn't known her sister all her life. They spent a lot of time together, chatting and just being sisters. When they were alone, Tendy told Cherish about her life outside; she told her all the good things about their father and about the fun they'd had when they were kids. She made sure Cherish knew she had a family out in the world, who loved her and would welcome her if she ever wanted to come and visit.

Her relationship with Dawn was different, and when they had time together, they'd talk about the community and their father. Dawn embraced the community ideology that Phil was the one who had wantonly sent his own father to prison, that Neville was utterly innocent and Phil wicked to make up such terrible stories about him. She had no reply when Tendy suggested that perhaps what had happened between their grandfather and their father was nobody else's business. What would happen, Tendy asked, if she stood up to Hopeful because she disagreed with him? Would the whole community hate her as well?

Whenever Dawn didn't have a counter-argument she would use the standard community tactic of quoting scripture or of twisting the meaning of the debate.

After her initial warmth, Sandy/Prayer kept herself aloof, apparently scared to get too close for fear her daughter would leave again.

Tendy had to have a wisdom tooth out while she was there. Dawn drove her into Greymouth for the appointment, with Tendy feeling conspicuous in the blue dress, until she realised that nobody knew her, and to the people of the town she was just another community person. She was still a smoker and had managed so far by sneaking out at night when nobody could see her, but the stress of the up-coming appointment got to her and she told Dawn she didn't care, but she needed a smoke. So there she was, wearing the long blue dress, puffing away on her cigarette, and laughing at the ridiculousness of the situation.

After the extraction she was in a lot of pain and needed strong medication. She woke the following morning with her mum stroking her face and saying, 'Come on, sweetie. Wake up now.' She felt that her mother had been standing watching her sleep. From then on, Sandy would let herself show that she did love her, and knowing that changed things for Tendy. Yes, there was all the hurt and nastiness, but now she knew absolutely that Prayer did love them all. She was able to talk to her mother about why she left them, and to ask her how she was able to do it. Prayer told her she'd asked Phil to let her have half the children, but he refused to split them up. When she got back from America she couldn't eat, she lost weight, and they had to take her to the doctor. But despite her distress she believed what she was doing was right because if she was in the community her children, too, would be saved. Hopeful taught that even if only one parent was in the community then the children would be granted eternal salvation.

Her only option as she saw it was to return to the community to serve God without her children; she had to do it to save them from damnation.

There was a family night while Tendy was there, when each family cooked their own special meal and went away to designated rooms to watch DVDs. Tendy, Prayer and Cherish cooked a feast. After they'd eaten they watched a DVD of Bible stories. The acting was as dire as the dress Tendy was wearing.

By the end of the first week she was exhausted from the mental strain of balancing the warmth and love against the full-on preaching. It was scary because she could feel part of herself being sucked in. She got frightened. What if she ended up not being able to leave? Yes, she'd have her mum and sisters, but to live their life of blind obedience? The thought horrified her and she told her mother she was going to leave at the end of the following week. Her life changed immediately. She wasn't allowed to be alone with Cherish and she had to spend two nights in a small caravan being preached at by Prayer and Dawn in a gentler version of the men's meetings. She handled it by going into sulky teenage mode: 'Okay. Whatever you say.' 'I don't give a shit, I just want this to be over.'

She kept repeating in her head: *I'm going. I'm going.*

At the end of the two weeks she changed back into her worldly clothes, folded the blue dress and left it behind along with her mother and sisters.

Her fortnight in the community turned out to be the best experience of her life, but the hardest as well. The good parts were discovering her mother did love them, learning about her early childhood, and Prayer giving her the teddy-bear that had been hers when she was little. The hardest part was cutting herself off again from the loving side of her mother, and she hated leaving Cherish.

Tendy returned to the world and went straight back to her old lifestyle. All the preaching and Bible-bashing she'd endured in the community made her wary of religion; she felt she needed to build her own self back up, and to do that she had to turn away from Christianity.

Israel, too, continued to live without God in his life. He graduated with two degrees from the University of Queensland with excellent grades and was courted by firms wanting to employ him. Instead, he worked in a café making cups of coffee and barely enough to live on. He'd never been so alone, estranged from his father, and out of touch with his siblings. His closest friend was the young man his father had objected to, but he was no substitute for family. Israel lost the faith that had been so important to him throughout his life and the future looked pointless and bleak. He was no nearer to understanding how God could have let such terrible things happen to their family.

Justine was in a happier situation, engaged to be married and secure in her faith. A problem arose when she discovered she had to have permission from both parents in order to marry at 19. She would have to ring the community to ask her mother to sign the papers, something she didn't want to do. Would Prayer agree and be happy for her, or would she preach at her and refuse?

In the end, there was no problem, since Prayer was happy to agree and Justine went ahead with the preparations, wondering all the time what it would be like to have her mother there to discuss things with. She had her bridesmaids, but she missed her mother, and her sisters. It was a struggle, trying to come to terms with the emotions of getting married without their support.

Her bridesmaids organised a trip to the West Coast for her hens' night, and while they were there they decided to visit the community. Justine and her cousin didn't go with them because they knew they'd be recognised and blow the girls' cover of being a university group. The others went, were welcomed, shown around and given lunch, but people got suspicious because of the photos they took and the questions they asked. Dawn took down the number plate of their car which happened to belong to Justine's future sister-in-law. The community did the research to find out who owned it, and a few days later, when Justine was round at her fiancé's house, Dawn rang asking to speak to Renee Van Kekem. Renee wasn't there, so Justine spoke to her instead, trying to get her head around the fact that Dawn was ringing her fiancé's house. Justine assured her that she had nothing to do with the visit and told her the girls must have just been curious. She thinks that the community must have been worried that another raid was planned.

The family gathered for the wedding. Phil, Bev, Crystal, Andreas, Mitchell and Jess flew in from Coffs Harbour. Israel and Tendy arrived from Brisbane. Prayer and Dawn stayed away.

Phil and Israel put up a good front for Justine's sake but, even so, Faith noticed that neither spoke to the other. She took Israel aside during the reception, telling him that he could come and live with them for a while if he would like to. He declined; living with his aunt was the last thing he wanted to do, but during the plane trip home her offer occupied his mind.

When Israel got back to Brisbane he saw that his dad was right, that there were aspects of manipulation and control in his relationship with his friend. The time away had given him a much clearer view, and he knew he needed to extricate himself. Going to New Zealand would be a good way out.

He rang to tell Faith he'd like to come. They welcomed him into their family and he stayed with them for 18 months.

Faith helped him talk about his past and to confront at last what he really felt about it. For the first time in his life Israel could be honest about how it had affected him. He'd arrived in Christchurch having lost everything – family, faith in God and his best friend. With nothing else to lose, he began the process of rebuilding from the start, learning to accept things rather than covering them up. Faith helped him confront his demons, one of which was the whole issue of control. She helped him see that he and his dad were repeating the pattern that Neville had set up, of love being conditional on obedience. They had each broken away by rebelling, but the rebellion left them estranged because that was the pattern they knew: *You are either with me or against me and there is no compromise.* Once Israel understood the concept of unconditional love, he was able to accept his dad as he was, without the frustration of needing to make him do things differently. Phil was who he was, and Israel found that it was possible to love him in spite of disagreeing with many of his ideas.

Under Faith's guidance Israel was able to mend his relationship with his dad, and also renew his contact with his siblings. She helped him understand more about the community and their beliefs, which in turn led him to an appreciation of free will and free choice. He saw that Sandy went back because she had to; the community didn't allow free will, but God did, so she was free to do what she believed to be the best for her children. Once he understood that, he was able to accept that God did still love them, and therefore there was hope of a brighter future. He started going to church again.

Faith's pragmatic approach appealed to Israel. Yes, some things were simply inexplicable and on those matters you just had to have faith in a loving God.

He got his life back on track, helped by his cousin who was instrumental in getting him a good job in a finance company. Eighteen months after he went to live with Faith, Israel got a promotion at work which would involve leaving Christchurch to live in Wellington. The prospect of leaving made him realise how much Justine's friend Jessica meant to him, and he asked her to marry him. At his wedding to Jessica Hooper early in 2007, Israel thanked Faith, saying that she had saved his life.

Tendy was also getting her life together. The turning point came when she was again in Brisbane and feeling at rock bottom. She rang her father, asking him to come up and visit her, not for money or for anything; she just needed to see him. He told her he was going to Thailand for business in a week's time but that he would see her before he went. She rang the next day, and the next. He promised again that he'd see her before he went, but he never came.

That broke her. She'd needed her dad and he wasn't there. But the effect was to make her decide she'd have to do things for herself. She was Phil's daughter and his strength and attitude in solving problems was ingrained, even though he'd let her down.

She put all her strength into action and sorted her life out, getting on top of her bills, ceasing to blame the community and her dad for her troubles, and learning to accept what had happened to her family. She drew on her two weeks with her mother, and could see that Prayer and Dawn were where they wanted to be. She felt she'd been able to say her piece about that and accept their point of view. She decided to let it all go and move on.

Tendy got a good job and is now in a stable, loving relationship. However because her partner was estranged from his wife, at first Phil didn't approve of the relationship and wouldn't condone it. Tendy felt excluded from the family. When she rang Phil, he was always busy, always in a meeting. It would have been easier to talk to the Pope. She felt steadier by now and though it didn't make her go into meltdown, it hurt, especially when she knew he spent hours talking to Justine, Israel and Crystal. Anything they wanted, he would get for them. Any time they wanted to talk, he would listen.

However, her father was doing some soul-searching of his own, and to his horror realised that he was following his father's pattern again, casting out a child who disagreed with him. He bought plane tickets and told Tendy he wanted them to come down so that he could meet Justin. That led to a two-hour phone call, when Phil simply shut up and let Tendy talk, which hadn't ever happened before, and she was able to tell him everything she'd been wanting to say for years. She told him she didn't want something to happen to him while they still had a bad relationship. Now when she rings up she gets put straight through, and is hopeful that their relationship will stay strong. All she wants from Phil is for him to listen when she rings up and talks to him about her life, the good parts and the bad.

CHAPTER EIGHTEEN:
REACHING OUT

*It seems that every time you try to forget about it or move on
with life it'll come up again; your mum will call, or your sister
will call, or you'll get a letter. So I just try and forget but it
doesn't work because I keep getting reminded.* Crystal

When she finished school at the end of 2006, Crystal wanted
to get away from Coffs Harbour. She was in a rut and
needed to spread her wings. She decided to begin a university
nursing course in New Zealand where she had plenty of family,
including Israel and Justine. Justine had left home when Crystal
was 13 and the sisters looked forward to reconnecting. But it was
Israel she'd missed the most: the brother who had been the anchor
of her childhood and was more a parent than a sibling.

Crystal didn't like being away from home and she missed her
dad, but she settled in, helped by living with Justine and Dion.
Early in the year there was also the excitement of the birth of their
daughter Annabelle.

Not long after Annabelle was born, Crystal was home by
herself when Dawn rang to chat to Justine about how she was
getting on with her new baby. With Gloriavale's expansion, the
hierarchy doesn't seem to exercise the same iron control over

communications with the outside – whether this is a deliberate policy or just a result of the dynamics of size, the Coopers don't know. The community is technologically advanced, using computers to keep track of their businesses and to communicate with clients. There are also computers in the school so that all the young ones grow up with technological expertise. There are phones throughout the accommodation blocks, used to communicate between the blocks and within the buildings. Some have access to outside lines.

On the day Dawn rang, Crystal ended up talking with her for about an hour and a half, chatting over family news including the birth of Dawn's son Loyal. But then the conversation changed. Dawn switched into a diatribe about how their grandad had gone to jail because of the lies people told about him. She said he was a martyr who was prepared to suffer for his faith and his community. She wanted Crystal to go to Gloriavale and stay for a week or two to see for herself what they were really like.

Crystal felt she already knew. To the community, her Christianity was a sadly diluted travesty of the real thing; they lived the one true life and believed that she would only find true Christianity with them in Gloriavale. She didn't even try to tell Dawn that, in her opinion, they lived in a box where they were controlled by Hopeful who pretty much acted as though he was God. She didn't accept the invitation.

Crystal began her nursing degree at university in Christchurch, working part-time in an old people's home to help support herself. But the community was never far away. Dawn rang again to speak to her about a programme her midwife had seen on television, where a young girl had said negative things about the community. Dawn said she was shocked to discover that Crystal was that girl and wanted to know what she'd said. Crystal told her that she'd only spoken the truth. She'd told the story of the visit where their mother had looked at them and said she wished now that she hadn't given birth to them.

Dawn couldn't deny what had been said because she had heard her mother, but she was sure she hadn't meant it like that. Crystal felt there was no other meaning to take from it. It was what it was. But as in her debates with Tendy, when Dawn was in a corner she twisted meanings or quoted from the Bible. Crystal knew it was useless to argue with her or to tell her she believed their mother abandoned them, because the community has such a stranglehold on the minds of its people.

Towards the end of the year, Crystal bumped into her Aunt Miracle and her husband Perry who were in Christchurch for the day, clad in their community uniforms. Shortly after that meeting, Crystal got a letter from her mother, the first contact Prayer had made since the disastrous visit several years before. The letter upset Crystal and she rang her dad. He read the copy she faxed him and told her not to take it to heart; it was living in the community that made her mother say the things she did; she didn't really mean them herself.

Sandy/Prayer's letter to her 'dearest Crystal' is a mix of a loving message to a lost daughter, a stark explanation of why she chose not to be her mother, and a dire warning to Crystal against her way of life. Crystal's chance meeting with Miracle and Perry had prompted Sandy to reach out to her daughter since it seemed God's way of telling her to make contact.

She had been delighted to hear from Miracle that Crystal looked like her – the only one of her seven children to do so. She was happy, too, that Crystal had chosen nursing as a career. Sandy had intended to work in an old people's home until she found 'greater fulfilment caring for the people of God'.

She explained how, when she was growing up, she stood up for her beliefs and how she was always searching for kindred spirits. She totally surrendered her will to God and found her spiritual home in the community Neville had created, committing herself to 'follow God and endure to the end'.

She wrote of her love for Phil 'and the wonderful man he was then', blaming his interest and involvement in business for his desertion of her and the community. Phil didn't know her very well, she asserted, if he believed the outsiders who assured him that once he had the children, she would follow him outside. Her family were only one part of her life and if it was God's will to allow her children to be taken from her, it was not for her to question God. She grieved but believed that Phil would realise his mistake and return with the children.

She prayed every day that God would take care of them. She believed that God was faithful, giving her Cherish in fulfilment of a promise made to her in a dream years earlier. Dawn had come back to her – further proof of God's mercy and faithfulness.

Sandy/Prayer touched on the disastrous visit in 2002 – as devastating for her as it had been for her children, however, the upsetting things had needed to be said: 'God never promised peace but a sword and that he would divide asunder to the heart and soul of a man.' The sight of her daughters had shocked her. They were so worldly, which meant they were ungodly. She wanted her daughters to be Godly women: 'Gentle and meek, dressed modestly as women of God should be.'

Yes, the visit had been a disaster for both sides, but the children had to know the danger they were in or their ungodliness would be their downfall. All she could do now was to pray to God for their salvation.

Prayer/Sandy wrote of her joy in Dawn and her family, and of her prayers that Cherish would grow up as she ought, despite being as headstrong as Justine had been.

God was real to Sandy/Prayer, whereas the Christianity of those who lived on the outside was powerless. The only proper way to serve God was to live for Him every minute of every day.

She hoped her letter would help Crystal understand. 'You were my little sunshine girl who loved to sit in the middle of the lounge with all the … song books around you, singing at the top of your voice.' She wished she could take the hurt away, go back and start again. But only stories ended in happy ever after.

'We have an enemy called the devil, and he is like a roaring lion, seeking whom he may devour. Only when Christ returns and we are taken to heaven will there be happy endings.'

She ends the letter with a blessing for her daughter, and the hope that Crystal will know the will of God in her life.

After a year in New Zealand Crystal was homesick for Australia and her father. She returned home and took up her studies again there.

Contact with the community continues and her lost family keeps reaching out but she, like the others, is wary of their motives. She doesn't remember Sandy being her mother and has never seen her motherly side during the few contacts they have had, but simply because she is her mother, her occasional forays into Crystal's life are disturbing.

She doesn't see Hopeful as her grandad. To her, he is the man who has wrecked the lives of many of his own children and grandchildren. She'd like to shake some sense into him, make him see what he's doing, and stop him controlling people and breaking their lives apart.

Phil and his children will always be connected to Gloriavale whether they like it or not. It's been a constant part of their lives and of the lives of Phil and Bev's daughter Jessica and Bev's son Mitchell. Jess at 11 is glad her dad left because otherwise she wouldn't have been born. Her religion is extremely important to her and she's grateful that she has the freedom to choose how to follow God. She's never been to the community but, because of what she has heard, feels that they have judged her dad harshly, and she knows he wouldn't do the things they accuse him of. As for being a Cooper: 'I love being in such a big family and having so many brothers and sisters. It makes life exciting. I'm an auntie now too and I really love that. There isn't one day that passes that isn't interesting. It's great being part of this family.'

Mitch, at nearly 16, also appreciates belonging to such a large family. 'The Cooper family is my family and I don't ever think of myself as an add-on. Sometimes I think about what life might have been like if I wasn't part of the family, and I'd probably be an only child instead of having all these brothers and sisters. I think I've got a broader outlook on life because of all the things we've been through and all the experiences we've had. It's been amazing to me to see what Phil has been through. I have respect for him when I hear how he struggled but prevailed after he came to Australia with nothing. In all ways, everything we do is a life-changing experience.'

But what has it been like for Bev, taking on a family with such a history and such ongoing entanglements?

'Being a part of the Cooper family is like a roller-coaster ride – both good and uncertain. There is always so much happening, and this draws many people into the family. Phil is so full of enthusiasm for life and for helping people. He loves having lots of people around him, which comes from his upbringing in a community and from having a large family himself.

'I like time to myself, and you certainly don't get that easily in such a big family, so I have struggled to cope with the magnitude of noise, mess and happenings. People often say to me, "You must be an amazing person to take on what you have." My reply is that I really must have been crazy, because who in their right mind would do this?

'My own family thought I was crazy, but I did it anyway. I knew early on that I was going to find it hard to cope, but by then I had a suspicion I could be pregnant. I remember thinking, If I'm not pregnant, I should run for my life, but if I am, I will stay and make this family work *somehow*!

'It has been a struggle to be a part of this family, but on the other hand I have grown to love all the Coopers so much. And with the kids already having lost one mother, how could I as a mother figure/friend leave them, too? I just couldn't do it, even though I was struggling to survive myself.

'It has been hard to watch Phil become more and more like his father. But even with all Phil's faults (and I have my own also), I have grown to love him so much.'

CHAPTER NINETEEN:
A NEW GENERATION

*We went to see Dawn when she was in hospital in Christchurch.
I knew Mum would be there, too, and there was this sense of
trepidation about seeing her again. I call it the community
feeling, it's a queasiness and an unrest in your stomach. But I was
excited, too, because I hadn't seen either of them for four or five
years. It's always strange to see them outside their own setting.
I don't think they feel it, but it feels odd to me.* ISRAEL

When Dawn was hospitalised in Christchurch at Easter 2008 because of problems with her second pregnancy, she rang Justine to say she'd love to see her. Justine knew her mother would be at the hospital, too, and she worried about how to greet her. She didn't think she wanted to hug her; Sandy/Prayer was a stranger.

Israel and Jess happened to be down in Christchurch with Zion their baby, so they all went to the hospital together which made it easier. Sandy/Prayer hugged Israel, then she hugged Jess and admired baby Zion. Justine sat down with 14-month-old Annabelle on her knee. Her mother didn't recognise her, which wasn't surprising since she looked very different from the last time Prayer had seen her. Her hair was longer, there was no nose ring, she wore a dress and glasses, but it felt odd not to be recognised by her own mother.

Eventually Prayer looked at her and asked, 'Is that you, Justine?' She made a comment about how she was all grown up, and things then settled down. Annabelle played with Dawn's son, Loyal; Dawn introduced her husband Abraham; and Prayer reminisced about what they'd all been like when they were little. It was information Phil hadn't known or passed on, and it showed a side of their mother that Justine and Israel had seen little of. The visit went well until Prayer began to preach at them when they got up to leave. 'What kind of a mother would I be,' she asked, 'if I didn't tell you about my religion and how I live?'

Justine kept her mouth shut. After the last time, when she'd spoken up and been shut down, she knew it wasn't worth the emotional stress of trying to stand up for her own views. However, Israel, articulate, intelligent and possessing an extensive knowledge of scripture, counteracted with his own views. Their mother didn't have the support of the community this time and was no match for her son. When she said they should live their lives the way she lived hers, he told her they should live the way Jesus lived his – after all, wasn't that the way they were all supposed to be living? He found it interesting that she didn't have an answer.

In the end, Prayer said she didn't want to finish on a bad note, but she had needed to let them know how she felt. And that was it, whereas, if she'd been in her own environment, Justine was sure, she would have kept going.

Justine and Israel were disappointed that Prayer had preached her sermon, but the pay-off of the visit was in seeing Dawn and meeting her husband and son. She was the same as she'd always been; she didn't deliver a sermon, and she was interested to hear all their news.

Prayer had seemed pleased to see her grandchildren. She held

Zion and let Jess take photos, but Annabelle wouldn't go to her, maybe because she sensed, as Justine did, that Prayer was holding herself aloof. However when they all said goodbye, Annabelle put both hands flat on her grandmother's face, and Prayer melted. Her maternal instincts might be buried deep but they were still there.

The next time Justine visited the hospital, she went by herself with Annabelle. She rang to tell Dawn she was coming and when she walked in, Prayer was just about to leave. She hadn't known they were coming and her face lit up. She sat back down and for the entire hour of the visit, talked normally. She seemed to have let her guard down and even though Justine suspected her mother was bitter inside, she didn't say anything negative about Phil and she didn't preach.

Justine met more of her extended family during the Easter break. She and Dion had arranged to go wake-boarding at Lake Brunner, but the accommodation there was booked out. Phil's brother John and his wife Maria put them in touch with Maria's mother, Toa Honour, who was no longer living in the community but spent a lot of time with her son Perry whose wife Miracle is Phil's sister. Although still part of the community, Perry and Miracle lived at Lake Brunner, having been given permission to live outside in order to support a teenage son who had been determined to leave. Some inside the community looked down on them because of this, but they had already had two sons leave, go off the rails completely, and end up in jail. If saving this son meant living outside the community, then they would do it. It can't have been an easy decision. Usually the cost of leaving was excommunication, and Perry held a senior position as business manager. However, perhaps because they weren't leaving in defiance of Hopeful, he gave his consent for them to live outside and to return to the community each day to work.

Toa Honour arranged for Justine and Dion to stay in the bach next to Perry and Miracle, and for the whole of Easter, Justine was able to get to know her aunt and cousins. Apart from Toa Honour, they all wore their blue dresses or shirts, but other than that, it was like being with an ordinary family. Justine loved it. All Miracle and Perry's nine children were there, except for the two eldest who were in prison. The son who wanted to leave was doing well and worked with Perry at the sphagnum moss plant.

Every day when Miracle got back from the community, Justine would go over to hang out and chat while Annabelle played with her cousins. She learned that her mother was in charge of the community kitchen and that the little girls were scared of her. They said that Prayer was very strict.

While they were away at Lake Brunner, Dawn's daughter was born without further complications. They named her Sweetly.

Justine went to visit Dawn before she left hospital. She arranged to meet her Grandma Naomi at the hospital, but when she got there, Prayer was outside talking to her, and Naomi was crying. Prayer took one look at Justine and demanded to know why she was wearing pants. She wasn't a man so why was she wearing a man's clothes? And look at Annabelle. Where was her dress?

Justine didn't bother answering.

Prayer turned to her mother. Why wasn't Naomi acting like a proper grandmother and telling Justine what she should wear?

Justine bit her tongue on retorting, *See what happens when you don't have a mother? You wear jeans!* It wasn't worth the hassle. Her mother was completely shut off. This time there was no light in her eyes and no warmth in her manner.

208

Prayer hadn't seen Naomi for five years and Justine wanted to shake her mother. She wanted to yell at her and tell her to look at herself. What was she doing preaching away at her own mother and making her cry?

Prayer refused to let them go up to the ward to see Dawn because people from the community were up there visiting. Then she added, 'But Dawn doesn't really care if you're there, anyway.'

Justine knew that wasn't true because it was Dawn who had rung her. Nevertheless, they went home without seeing the baby or Dawn again. Justine suspected that her mother didn't want the community people to know of her own contact with Justine and Naomi, or to see her worldly relatives.

One evening while Dawn was in hospital, Justine got a phone call from Cherish. She spoke as if she knew Justine well. 'Hi, Justine, it's Cherish here. I was just wondering if I could see you – I'm coming to Christchurch to see Dawn and I'd really like to see you.'

Justine wanted to see her, too, but the time of the visit clashed with when Justine cared for pre-schoolers in her home. Cherish said it didn't matter because she'd be down again, but that turned out to be the day Prayer wouldn't let Justine and Naomi visit. Justine was disappointed. She'd wanted to meet the sister their mother said was so like her in looks and personality.

It's always a balancing act for the Coopers where the community is concerned. Any contact with Prayer could go either way, or be a mix of motherliness and preaching. Her children have all come to an accommodation: she is their mother, but not their mother. They've come to realise that they'll never be able to leave the community behind because those inside keep reaching out to them, or they'll see them in town in their blue dresses, or there will be a documentary on television.

There's always the tension between what the community believes and their own beliefs. Tendy is the only one who no longer goes to church. The others have chosen their spiritual paths of their own free will, something that they value having been able to do. Their mother and sisters haven't had the chance to choose for themselves; they've never had to think about what they believe, they've never questioned it or asked if it was right. Once you're inside the community, as Tendy experienced, you are told what is right and your own opinions and ideas are challenged until you accept the 'right' way of thinking. Dawn, as a troubled and very young teenager, wouldn't have had a hope of standing out against the indoctrination.

None of them is bitter about what their mother did in abandoning them to return to the community. They know how strong the pull is and Tendy has seen at first hand how deeply they believe in their faith. Their mother is who she is; she has her own beliefs and they have theirs. They accept that they will never agree with her when she tells them the Bible teaches that they should be living the way the community lives. Justine wonders just which Bible the community is reading.

For Israel, each visit to the community has been something of an emotional ordeal because of the intensity of judgements and accusations fired at visitors. He has found himself dealing with it for weeks afterwards because a lot of what's said is good and right, which plants a seed of doubt. He knows the dark side, though, and is very aware of how they twist things, so he prefers to stay away.

In mid 2008, all the family except Phil were sent invitations to attend the biennial concert season, held over three weeks at

Gloriavale. Dawn rang Crystal and Andreas, urging them to come and stay on for a few days afterwards. Andreas didn't want to go. Crystal thought that just going to the concert would be enough. She didn't promise that she would go, but she would think about it. In the end, only Israel and his family attended. He went with the usual feelings of trepidation, but this visit was a healing one. He and his wife and son stayed the night and spent time with Prayer and Cherish. Like Tendy, he was amazed at how Cherish felt like the sister he'd known all his life. He loved meeting her and was thrilled that she wanted to spend time with him and his family and get to know as much about them as she could.

The best thing was talking with his mother. Early in the visit, he cleared the air by telling her he wanted her to know that he didn't hold anything against her and that he forgave her for leaving them.

Her answer gave a hint of what her decision had cost her. 'I know you do, Israel. I only wish all your sisters did.' She went on to explain and justify her decision until he told her to stop; he accepted what she'd done and her reasons for it. It seems, though, that she is no more at peace with what happened than Phil is. Sandy chose the name Prayer because prayer was all she had left. Praying for her children was all she could do for them.

Any uneasiness Israel had anticipated diminished and faded entirely as the visit progressed. His mother didn't lecture him, which allowed him to see her as a person rather than as a community member. He saw the positive side of Gloriavale and almost felt he could live that way because there was so much that appealed. He knew, though, that he would never want to give up the freedom to make his own world, to be able to test himself, make mistakes and learn from them. His mother and Dawn were happy to be where they were, but he was glad Phil had taken him out. He was also pleased that he and Jess had made the effort to visit, and that they were allowed to talk to Prayer without Hopeful hovering over them. His grandfather left them alone for the entire time, perhaps because he was too busy with the concert, at which Oscar-winner Richard Taylor of Weta Workshop was a star attendee. Hopeful had swelled with pride as he introduced him to the audience. It was to Weta Workshop that three members of the community had been sent several years earlier to learn how to construct the props and special effects used in the concerts.

The concerts are big events on the Coast. Retirement homes take busloads of their residents and families come from the surrounding district. The concert is styled as a love-gift for the local community.

The dining hall is taken over for the season and decorated with elaborately painted hangings representing the theme, which in 2008 is the Rainforest Express. The walls are covered with a painted forest, the stage framed with trees on which toucans and other birds perch. A couple of lizard-like creatures respond to sound so that they bounce up and down when Hopeful strides the stage, preaching his version of the ideal family life to his captive audience. The musical performances are polished and flawless, the singing likewise. The skits are non-religious and funny but they are reminiscent of school concerts of the fifties. And all the while, girls in long blue dresses and headscarves serve the three-course meal. They have names such as Serenity, Hope, Mercy, Rapture, Angel. Other young women come quietly in and stand at the side holding their babies and watching for a few minutes. They all look like teenagers but some have several children.

During the concert, Hopeful gets two boys to carry a large photo onto the stage and while they hold it up he explains that none of the children in that photo would have been born if Gloriavale was like the outside world and believed that two children were enough. According to him, the community loves children; they welcome them; they look after them.

A phenomenal amount of effort goes into the concert. As well as the model train on stage, there is a miniature railway running around the back of the hall, built entirely by the community except for the engine. At dramatic moments in some of the items, the lights dim, the thunder rolls, and the floor beneath the audience moves up and down. The science teacher who introduces himself as Faithful, opens the play based on the story of Noah, fluently explaining for some minutes that the flood was a real event that produced the fossils of the world which in turn prove that the theory of evolution is wrong. Then the actors build an ark for the animals which parade in: a life-sized and beautifully constructed elephant, two camels, two ponies, a couple of rhinos, a lion, a cow and several other creatures. Everything looks professional. Everything has been made by the community.

The whole concert appears to be controlled by Hopeful. He is 82, the same age as the Pope, but the contrast in vigour between the two men is startling. Hopeful leaps around the hall, untroubled by the stairs. He watches everything and moves about the room, making his presence felt. A young mother standing by the wall with her baby sees him looking at her and scuttles away. He wants more light on the stage and calls out an order. The lights come up immediately.

At the end of the concert, Hopeful takes the stage again to explain that they don't take anything from the audience; instead, they give each person a gift. On the visitors' way out, girls of about ten hand out loaves of homemade bread and pats of butter. The girls keep their eyes lowered. They give the impression that they are schooling their features to conceal their shock at the sight of the worldly, immodestly dressed people they are serving.

Gloriavale is a conundrum. The little children playing outside under the supervision of the pre-school teachers look like miniature adults in their long blue dresses and headscarves, or blue trousers and shirts. It is like looking through a time-warp at the American pilgrims. But the people of Gloriavale look happy. They care for each other; they have purpose, shelter and fellowship. The teenagers know how to work and don't get into trouble. But everyone is tied there by indoctrination and economics. If they leave, they leave with nothing, and how do you live in the outside world if you know nothing about it, have no money and a big family to support?

It looks pure and modest and seemly, but in the town, people speak of the Gloriavale men renting pornographic movies in the past. Do they still? Phil believes a leopard doesn't change its spots and, by some accounts, the environment is still highly sexualised. One man reported in 2007 how at breakfast, Hopeful would ask, 'Okay men, hands up those who fucked their wives last night.'

The man telling the story saw nothing wrong with that. Hopeful was helping his followers be more open about sex. It is difficult to see how such an attitude fits with the modest clothing and the demand for purity before marriage.

What will happen to Gloriavale when Hopeful Christian dies, or becomes incapable of leading? Some say it will keep going, that there are strong men who will step up, who have led it before when Hopeful was in prison – although he was apparently still very much in control even then, with daily phone calls and regular visitors. Others hope that with his death will come the opportunity for the community to fulfil its potential as a place of true Godliness. But whatever leadership follows, there are many who will be devastated when their current leader dies.

The story of the Cooper family continues to unfold. September 2008 brought more contact with the community. Sandy, Dawn and Cherish rang several times to speak to Crystal and Andreas, urging them again to fly over, go to the concert and stay a few days. Yes, the concert season had ended but Hopeful said to tell them they would put on a special performance, just for the two of them.

Neither wished to attend and they didn't want to talk to their mother either if she was the one to ring. Crystal tries to talk to her and wants to have a proper mother-daughter conversation, but feels that when she talks to Sandy she gets no loving, motherly response. Andreas has thought about what a mum would be like, and he likes the idea of having one, but when she phones, he too feels there's nothing there.

When the caller ID showed that the September call was coming from New Zealand, Andreas ran from the room, refusing to answer. Phil picked it up, and thought he was speaking to Dawn, but it was Cherish. It was a powerful moment, hearing his daughter's voice. 'Wow! Honey, this is so nice – the first time I've ever spoken to you.' He couldn't believe that what he had hoped for since he discovered her existence was actually happening.

She was reserved to start with, telling him it wouldn't be possible for them to meet unless he came to live in Gloriavale. Then she started crying, saying she'd always wanted to have a dad like everyone else in Gloriavale.

Phil said she'd probably heard a lot of bad things about him, but that there were two sides to every story.

'What about Grandad? And why did you leave me?'

He assured her that what had happened between Neville and him had nothing to do with her. As to why he left her, she needed to ask her mum. 'Ask her to tell you what's on your birth certificate. It says "father unknown", but your mum knows the truth.'

Cherish told him how much she would have loved to be part of a big family, to have brothers and sisters – but only Dawn was a Christian. The others weren't, they didn't walk with God.

'Don't judge as you've been told,' Phil said. 'Judge as you see.'

Sandy/Prayer took the phone then and began talking to him, something she hadn't done since she'd left America. She didn't accuse him outright of influencing Crystal and Andreas to stay away from her and the community, but he got the strong impression that she believed it. The conversation was fairly predictable. Phil found it interesting that she wasn't able to grasp that each of the kids was their own person, that they made up their own minds. Phil believes that Sandy and Neville are so used to Neville making the decisions that neither of them understands that Phil's children have the freedom to act according to their own beliefs and wishes – that Neville assumes Phil is the same as him in controlling every aspect of his children's lives. But Phil also believes that at the same time, Neville is trying to win the children back, now that they are old enough to defy their father.

Neither Crystal nor Andreas went to the concert. They say they might go over one day and spend time with their family. Both would love to see Dawn again, and get to know Cherish. About their mother they're not so certain. They'd like to be able to relate to her as a mum, but they haven't yet felt any reaching out from her. Not from her heart, anyway.

The family all hope that Gloriavale will change with time to become a place of true Godliness where people choose freely to stay or go. Their mother, Dawn, and Cherish are happy there and all the 'outside family' want is to be able to visit freely and for the community family to be able to visit them without penalty or preaching. They hope the community will open its doors and allow contact with the outside world so that those who have been born inside can judge for themselves where they want to live. They see the Hutterite model as the ideal: a community that lives apart from the world while retaining links to the outside – a community which doesn't shun those who leave.

There is much about Gloriavale that is good and admirable. That alone, the family believes, should be enough to draw people to live there of their own free will.

Justine's wedding day, Christchurch, 2004. Left to right: Andreas, Tendy, Israel, Crystal, Justine holding Jessica, Mitchell.

CHAPTER TWENTY:
TIME FOR REFLECTION

*Until now, I've never had time to figure out who or what
I am. I've always had a plan; I'm never happy unless I'm
busy. Part of me is still running – I'm not sure what from,
but being busy is all I know how to do.* PHIL

For Phil the story isn't finished and he admits that it might never be. His children have achieved a certain peace about their mother leaving them, although it gets shaken every time the community reaches out to them. His own relationship with his children is changing. Now that they are adults he has found he can be more open with them about how events impact on him. He can ask them for support instead of feeling he must always appear strong and invulnerable.

Phil's challenge now lies in dealing with the damage from his past, something he's been able to avoid so far in the hurly-burly of the life he created for himself. Part of what he has to deal with is the inheritance from his father, both in his characteristics and his way of relating to others. He strives not to be like his father and has succeeded in many important ways, one of the most crucial being that his children haven't had to suffer the abuse that he did. But he's aware, too, that his father's legacy is insidious; he continually has to fight to keep the difficult side of his own personality in check and he doesn't always win that battle. Sometimes he finds himself reacting to situations in exactly the same way as his father would do, and it shakes him. As with Neville, Phil likes to be the one calling the shots and it isn't always easy to give up that power. A history like his must leave emotional scars, some of which will probably never be healed. He knows that as a family they all need more time to heal. It's a slow process and Phil has never been used to going slowly. He understands that in many ways he's very like his father, but the difference is that Phil doesn't want to be like Neville. He is determined to stop the sins of his father from being visited on the next generation and on those still to come.

Did he do the right thing in taking the children out of the community? They have definite opinions on the question which has haunted him for the past 18 years.

Israel: 'I'm sure Dad'll question that till the day he dies because regardless of what he sees in us and what we say to reassure him, he still asks: Did I do the best thing for my children? Maybe I should have just let them go back to the community with their mother.

'The day our mum left was a huge day that's continued to have resounding repercussions for my dad and for all of us. Should he just have given up and let us go with our mum? I'm sure they would have had that conversation – I'm sure Dad could have done that if he'd thought that was the best thing. There would have been very different outcomes for all of us kids.

'Definitely, I think he made the right choice. I think it's better to have freedom and the ability to understand and to make your own choices. And that's what we've done – we've chosen, all of us at different times, to go back into the community and see her; none of us were ever forced. It's better to be able to choose to go and see it, than be forced to live there and have no freedom to choose your way of life.

'Most of us have come to find faith and belief in God, as our mother so dearly wanted us to. We understand clearly that our teachers in matters of faith are, like us, human and fallible. All of us seek to know the word of God; none of us claims to be the ultimate authority. This in itself is testament to the power of choice.'

Justine: 'I'm definitely glad Dad took me out. Definitely. He sometimes gets real upset and tries to apologise for taking us away from our mother. But I wouldn't have wanted it any other way if that's what it took to get out of there. I'd rather be out than be with my mum because I didn't know her. She's a stranger, so it's not as big for me. Why would you say sorry? I can see where Dad's coming from because he did take us away from her. But weighing it up, I'm pleased I'm out. I don't know what I'd be like or who I'd be married to if I was still in there.

'Dad's my hero. I love him. I'm the most protective person of my dad.'

Tendy: 'In the end, after going to the community, I said to Dad, "Yes, we've all made mistakes." It's just that he's never forgiven himself. I think he still questions if he made the right decision. I asked him all these questions – why this and why that – and I said, "Dad, you've got to move on. You've got to put the past in the past and leave it there." I think that's been the hardest thing for me, every time I go home or we're together, the community is the thing that comes up. It's always about the community. I know there's a lot of hurt with my family towards the place but I don't have any hurt towards them. Yes, I wish my grandad wasn't there and Mum was out, but I don't hate the place.

'I think Dad always thinks he's never given us enough. But being older now, I don't regret anything. I loved the way I was brought up – I've lived with friends who didn't even know how to do the washing. And we were all washing our clothes and doing the cooking when we were seven. I look at that now and I appreciate it. At the time I hated it, but now I look back and go wow! I'm at the stage where I really like who I am and if that all didn't happen, or the crap that I had to get myself into to finally wake up to myself hadn't happened, I don't think I'd be who I am now. I said that to Dad and said I just want to be able to ring him up and tell him all my crap whether he cares about it or not, and for him to say, "I love you, Tendy."

'I'm pleased that he took us out and gave us that option. Maybe our life could have been different – all the hurt and all the mistakes that we made, we might have prevented all that. But I'm not sad that it's happened. In a way, it was supposed to happen. He gave us the choice. I'm glad that he did.'

Crystal: 'Dad asks us the question and we always say, "No, Dad – we're happy to be out of that place."

'When we were younger we'd probably have said, leave us with Mum, but you have to be older to see that it was a good thing that he took us away. It was better for us, otherwise we'd still be in there, still living the way they live and having no realisation of life. They have the same thing every day. I feel sorry for them. They don't experience life. They don't go out and experience anything that God has created.

'Dad did the right thing when he took us out. I love my dad. I've always been close to him. When we were little I grew up with my dad – the older kids miss Mum more than I do because I didn't really know her even though everyone says I look like her. My grandma tells me that all the time.

'Dad's made mistakes in his life – but everybody has and we've all done stuff we regret. He's a good man and he's got a big heart. He cares – he probably cares too much about some things. He's very generous, and he's like – my dad.'

Andreas: 'I'm definitely glad I'm not in there. It's too controlled. I wouldn't mind the work, but I wouldn't like never being able to travel, always having someone watch you, never meeting new people or never having a fire on the beach – never *going* to the beach.

'I've heard about it all through Dad and through all the stories, but it's been easy for me. I know how he saved us, how he worked hard and started with nothing. He made the right choice and he gave Mum the choice. He did the right thing and he rose up. He's been like a mum and a dad.'

Their answers are unequivocal. They like who they are; they enjoy being able to make their own way in the world and to chart their own courses. They value very highly having been able to choose for themselves how to live and what to believe. They know their father isn't perfect, but they love him and want him in their lives.

And what of Cherish, the daughter Phil's never been able to meet? In 2008 Prayer rang to say that Cherish would like to talk to him. It was something he'd yearned for ever since he'd heard of her birth. Speaking to him by accident when she'd rung last time had apparently helped Cherish to realise that he was an ordinary person and not a monster. They spoke for some time, with her asking the questions and him doing his best to answer them truthfully. Whether he'll ever be able to meet her he doesn't know, but at least he has spoken to her and that is a memory he treasures.

At the end of 2008 Cherish was sent with Sandy for three months to India to be part of the community outpost there. Phil thinks that the community saw it as a way to direct her restlessness. On the other hand, there is apparently no suitable young man at Gloriavale for her to marry, partly because Hopeful has decreed that cousins may not marry and the only available young men are her cousins. Phil is still hoping that one day he will be able to meet her, but knows it is unlikely to happen while his father is alive. He doesn't want Cherish to go through life without having a relationship with her father.

However his relationship with his own father may never be resolved because of Neville's refusal to have any contact with his son.

Phil wrote the following letter to his father, in the hope that Neville will one day read it.

Dear Dad,
There is so much I want to tell you and say to you. As I can never ring or talk to you I thought I would try and write.
Dad, I know there are many times I have hurt you and I know I have disappointed you in not being the son you wanted, but like you I have gone my own way. The saddest thing with that is that you have turned your back on me and your grandchildren. It has been nearly 10 years since I tried to talk to you when I flew over to see you in prison. All I wanted to say is 'I'm sorry if I have done wrong' but you would not even give me two minutes and you turned your back on me. I know you blame

me for sending you to prison but Dad, you know the truth. If only you hadn't been so proud and stubborn you could have spoken to all the victims who laid those charges and you could have made right what you did. But you chose to deny it. Dad, you know the truth. For what you did to me, I forgive you. We must all live with our own conscience; remember that. There is so much more I could say and would like to say, but it would take many, many pages so I will leave it, hoping that one day you will pick up the phone and just say, Hi, son. Love, Your son, Philip.

Phil knows it is unlikely that Neville/Hopeful will ever willingly speak to him again, but it doesn't stop him hoping and wishing things could be different. On the other hand, he's proud of what he's done with his life in the years since he left the community. He's proud, too, of his children. He has reason to be. They are extraordinarily resilient, forgiving and forward-looking. They are intelligent, lively and attractive.

He deeply appreciates the strong relationship he now has with his oldest son. Israel is a remarkable young man: fresh-faced, and energetic, with a zest for life that seeks out challenges just for the thrill of overcoming them. That desire for action, and the appetite for problem-solving is strong in the Cooper gene-pool – Faith has it, as do Phil and Israel. Israel also has the Cooper determination and strength of character. Like Faith, he needs to analyse and research situations so that he understands them. He knows the destruction that determination and strength of character can wreak if not constantly monitored and used as a force for good.

Phil mourns the loss of Dawn, and that he can't be a grandfather to her children. Watching Justine, he marvels at the brilliant mother that she is. He wonders how this young woman who lost her own mother before she was five years old learnt such nurturing skills. He believes it is her inheritance from Sandy, part genetic and part memory.

Of all Phil and Sandy's children, Tendy travelled the most difficult road to adulthood, by her own admission messing up her teenage years. While life now isn't always smooth, she faces the future with hope, humour and energy – and the knowledge that she's deeply loved by her family.

Phil's relationship with Crystal and Andreas has been the least fraught; they don't remember their mother being with them as children and, in that sense, adjusting to life without her was easier. For them, their dad was always the only parent, with Israel a constant, reliable and comforting presence in their lives. As the youngest, they also benefited most from Bev's presence in the family.

Phil himself is positive, forward-looking and jumping with vitality, and his message is simple: go forward, your destiny is in your own hands. He has seen how bitterness and hate can twist lives and wants none of that for his own children. However, for them the warning doesn't seem necessary. They have inherited his own determination to lead good and productive lives.

With his children pretty much grown up, and what he set out to do with his business achieved, Phil was ready for a new challenge. Between them, he and Israel decided it was time to tell their story. They felt there was enough distance from the searing events of the past to look back and get them in some perspective. They had seen that people were fascinated whenever they related one of the hundreds of extraordinary episodes that make up their history.

For Phil, it was important to show what happened; he wasn't

interested in glorifying himself or vilifying Neville or the community. He wanted others to see that it's possible to take control of your own life, and keep getting up again no matter how many times you are knocked down.

He knew that setting his life down on paper would mean having to reach back into painful memories, something he had so far been able to avoid because of the way he lived his life. His way of coping, and of caring for his family, has always been to go forwards, to act rather than to look inward or analyse.

Telling the stories was often distressing, stirring up emotions he'd never dealt with. But laying it out it has clarified things for him, and has given his children a deeper understanding of their childhood.

'My perspective keeps changing. Ten years ago I would have had more bitterness, more wanting to lay blame. One thing I've learnt is that blaming others for your troubles never helps.'

His story is what it is. The important thing, he says, isn't the hand you're dealt in terms of parents and upbringing; it's what you do with that hand. If Phil and the Cooper children had a motto, it would probably follow the spirit of Proverbs 3:15 which discusses wisdom. Theirs would read: '*Freedom of choice* is more precious than rubies: and all the things thou canst desire are not to be compared unto that.'

The Coopers know that most people take freedom of choice for granted. However, the freedom to chart one's own path isn't something any of this family will ever take lightly. They live in hope that their Gloriavale family will one day be able to make at least some of their own decisions about how they live their lives.

The story is not complete, as Phil knows only too well. Even during the year of writing, so much happened; family dynamics changed, children were born, tentative contact was made between both branches of the family.

But Phil hopes that, above all, his story will inspire.

'I believe you can turn your life around and make the most of it; you have the power to do it, not anyone else. You choose your own feelings. This is not a sad story but one of hope; yes, it's a story of struggle but through struggle comes strength.'

Dedications from Phil to his family:

'I want to say thank you to Mum and Dad for giving me life. What I do with that life is my choice. How I let my upbringing affect me is also my choice.

'To my beloved children: always try to see the good in people. I'm glad I gave you freedom of choice. I'm proud of all of you. I haven't been the best dad in the world, but I hope you will be able to give your kids more time than I was able to give you. Go out and make a difference in this world, always reach out to your fellow man and fulfil your God-given dreams.

'To my grandchildren: Grandad loves you all very much; may your dreams be big. As you grow older and read our story, I hope you will understand that in life we have struggles, but you at least have freedom.

'To Sandy, thank you for being part of my life and bringing into the world our beautiful children. I know you love them.

'To my children and grandchildren whom I have never met: if you ever read this, know that I love you. Dream big and never be controlled by any man. Reach out and become the person God wants you to be.'

Israel and his wife Jess at their wedding – Christchurch, January 2007.

Acknowledgements

I wish to thank the following people.

Fleur Beale who spent 14 months trying to get me to sit down long enough to put this together. You have done an amazing job.

To Bev, my wife for the past 13 years, who took on six kids and me, which makes seven kids. Thank you for being part of our lives. Thank you Mitch, you were two years old when you joined this full-on family and you are now very much part of us.

To my brother John and my sisters Faith and Mercy, thank you for your support and help throughout the years.

To my late brother Michael, thank you for your friendship, support and laughter. You are always in our thoughts.

To the Wenborn family, thank you for your support in the early years.

To Wes and Ellen Anderson, thank you for giving so much of your love. Your gift of the use of the bach in the Sounds made so much of this possible.

To Melanie Reid from TV3, thank you for your courage in helping bring this story to life through your documentaries, and for your willingness to experience the pain and struggle with us.

To my dear friends in America, the Hutterite people who helped so much: thank you for three wonderful years.

To all the many others who helped us in so many ways: thank you.

Lastly to my children: thank you for being who you are. This journey with all its ups and downs has often been difficult, but we are stronger for the experience.

I love you all.

Phil Cooper